# THE
# LODGE MENTOR

Richard Johnson

D1600946

Lewis Masonic

First published 2010

ISBN 978 0 85318 339 6

Published by Lewis Masonic

an imprint of Ian Allan Publishing Ltd, Shepperton, Middx TW17 8AS.
Printed in England.

Visit the Lewis Masonic website at www.lewismasonic.co.uk

# Contents

|  | Foreword | 5 |
| 1. | Introduction | 6 |
|  | Mentoring from the Candidate's Viewpoint | 10 |
|  | Characteristics of a Mentor | 12 |
| 2. | The Candidate for Initiation | 21 |
| 3. | The Member after Initiation | 26 |
|  | Introduction | 26 |
|  | Recalling the Degree Ceremony | 27 |
|  | Presentation | 27 |
|  | Obligation and Demonstration | 31 |
|  | Explanation | 33 |
|  | Aftermath | 38 |
| 4. | The Member after Passing | 44 |
|  | Introduction | 44 |
|  | Recalling the Degree Ceremony | 45 |
|  | Presentation | 45 |
|  | Obligation and Demonstration | 46 |
|  | Explanation | 48 |
|  | Aftermath | 51 |
| 5. | The Member after Raising | 55 |
|  | Introduction | 55 |
|  | Recalling the Degree Ceremony | 58 |
|  | Presentation | 58 |
|  | Obligation and Enactment | 58 |
|  | Demonstration and Explanation | 59 |
|  | Aftermath | 62 |
| 6. | The Member en route to the Master's Chair | 69 |
| 7. | The Member after Occupying the Master's Chair | 79 |

| | | |
|---|---|---:|
| 8. | Handing over the Duties of Lodge Mentor | 84 |
| | Appendix | 87 |
| | The Workings of the Lodge | 87 |
| | Lodge Officers | 87 |
| | Warrant of the Lodge | 98 |
| | Lodge Summons and Literature | 99 |
| | Toasts at the Festive Board | 101 |
| | The Workings of Provincial Grand Lodge | 103 |
| | The Workings of Grand Lodge | 109 |
| | The Major Masonic Charities | 115 |
| | The Freemasons' Grand Charity | 115 |
| | Royal Masonic Benevolent Institution | 117 |
| | Royal Masonic Trust for Girls and Boys | 119 |
| | Masonic Samaritan Fund | 122 |
| | The Charity Festivals | 124 |
| | Acknowledgements | 126 |
| | About the Author | 128 |

# Foreword

I was honoured when Richard asked me to write an introduction to his book which I believe will be a valuable resource for the Masonic Mentor. Richard has brought together a wide range of subjects which will be a great help to mentors in their work with new masons.

In this book Richard has been able to go into considerable detail about the meaning of our ceremonies, the work of the four central Charities and an overall approach to Mentoring in general. He has drawn on his considerable Masonic experience both in this country and the United States, not only to look at the mechanics of being a Masonic Mentor, but also to explain some of the symbolism in our ceremonies which so often mystifies our new members.

Being a Masonic Mentor is in essence a very simple concept. His task is to make the new brother feel welcome, involved and at home in his Lodge and introduce him to Freemasonry in general. However, this last part of his work is such a huge subject that no one person can know everything about it and so the mentor needs a great deal of support. Providing this support is one of the objects of the mentoring schemes being set up throughout the United Grand Lodge of England.

I am sure that mentors will find this book an important addition to their library and a useful reference in their work.

James Bartlett
October 2009

# Introduction

The concept of the office of mentor has been discussed in Masonry for some time. In several lodges the role has been carried out for many years by members, albeit not necessarily in a formal sense. Recently Grand Lodge made the decision to create a mentor's jewel for a Provincial Officer, which is shown on this page, and several Provinces have appointed Provincial and Group mentors at their annual meetings. They have also produced booklets and other leaflets with information to all people involved in the mentoring scheme. Some of these Provinces have been recommending to their lodges for the last few years that they formally appoint a lodge mentor, and so the concept is currently growing in acceptance.

One of the questions to be asked at the outset of reading this book is "Why bother; why now?" Lodges have been in existence for over 300 years, so why should one create this new position? Some would say that the proposer and seconder should look after their candidate Masonically from cradle to grave, or certainly until he has the confidence and experience to make his way unaided. Some would say that the Director of Ceremonies of the lodge and his assistant should be looking after all members. Others might say that the Secretary or Almoner of the lodge, who each interact with all of the membership, should take ownership of this duty. Most lodge members will probably say they think it is someone else's job. And yet if you check the addresses given to these Officers when they are appointed at an installation meeting, it is obvious that this potential aspect of their work has not been specifically expressed.

One area of common ground covered in some of the existing mentoring notes is the need to avoid the onset of disillusion in the new Mason, and comments recorded from those who have left or nearly left the Craft after a short time have included:

- I wasn't sure exactly what I was joining;
- I wasn't sure what the three ceremonies were about;
- I felt embarrassed that I couldn't answer the questions from my family and friends;
- I was confused why I had to leave a later lodge meeting (going into a higher degree).
- The other members seemed to have stable and exclusive cliques with their friends.

If any of these comments were to come from one of our newer members, are we surprised when after a time he does not turn up to lodge meetings, and then after more time leaves altogether? The increased focus on mentoring is partly as a result of these types of comments being reported more frequently, and the Province Grand Lodges wishing to be more pro-active in improving the system that is in some way failing.

This mentoring concept is sometimes described as being aimed at recruitment, retention and retrieval, the three Rs. The middle one is seen as the most important, because of the relatively high proportion of new Masons that resign from the Craft in the first five or so years. If retention can be addressed in a positive way, then retrieval should become less of a problem. While we know that some people come into Masonry and find out quickly that it is not for them, and we will not alter their intention to depart, the majority of relative newcomers who are thinking of leaving the Craft would probably cite some or all of the reasons given in the previous paragraph. And the best method of addressing these issues is education, which may be why the chisel has been chosen as the jewel for this office.

Many commercial organisations run induction courses for newcomers who have recently joined them. These are designed to help them to familiarise themselves with their new surroundings, not only to understand the organisation they have joined, but to introduce them to the customs, practices and routines that are adopted therein. Very often there are additional training courses, not just aimed at the organisation's requirements, but which are educational for them in a wider context. Compare that with the concept in some lodges that the three degrees are self explanatory, and the newcomer will pick up the other aspects by watching and listening as everyone has done previously. So perhaps the call for mentoring is trying to address what in many other organisations would be considered a less than optimum introduction to a new way of life.

Also it has to be admitted that candidates enter lodges these days by various routes. No longer is it the case that every candidate has a proposer and seconder who have known him for several years, and who can undertake the supervision of his welfare. Admittedly some come in as a result of family connections, others have interacted with Masons at work or socially, while some have read books or seen films about Masonry which have prompted their interest – there is a variety of ways into our organisation, so the approach perhaps has to have a degree of flexibility to cope with these variations.

Sometimes the candidate may know the proposer well, perhaps at work or via some other mutual activity, and someone else in lodge agrees to be the seconder without any particular prior knowledge of him – this candidate then has only one personal supervisor available who knows him well. Some candidates offer themselves for Freemasonry after interacting with the Craft by their own researches, perhaps via open lodge and other meetings or via the internet, and they come to a lodge without anyone having some personal knowledge of them. So in modern times it is sometimes useful to have the fallback of a lodge mentor or similar person to step forward and take the new man under his wing.

Lodges have in the past assumed the different aspects of mentoring in several ways. Some lodges have the tradition that the Entered Apprentices are to be supervised by the Junior Warden, and the Fellowcrafts by the Senior Warden, and presumably the Master Masons by the Master himself or possibly delegated to the Immediate Past Master. In other lodges the Senior Warden has covered all members below the rank of a lodge Officer. Thus at every stage of a Mason's career, up to the Master's chair or at least being an Officer, there was someone in lodge monitoring his progress and offering guidance where required. Thereafter the Mason should probably have enough knowledge and contacts to take care of himself.

Already some lodges traditionally send someone out when Entered Apprentices or Fellowcrafts are requested to leave the lodge while a higher degree is worked for another lodge member, or at an installation when Master Masons and below are asked to step outside the lodge for a time. This person may be a Grand Officer or somebody senior and of great experience, or might be a more junior member or a Steward of the lodge who quite recently himself was asked to step outside of the lodge for a time, and could therefore interact as more of an equal with the juniors.

The lodges cited as examples in the last two paragraphs will probably encounter little resistance in accommodating the Provincial Grand Lodge request for a formal lodge mentor to be appointed. Other lodges may not be totally on board with the need for this new appointment, but perhaps after reading this book they may agree that there are benefits to be gained by such appointments in the future, or at least informally adopting some of the concepts.

It should be noted that in this book there are repeated references to 'Province' and 'Group'. Confusion can arise when collections of lodges overseas are called 'Districts' and are essentially equivalent to the UK Provinces, and that some Provinces use the terminology 'District' or even 'Division' instead of 'Group' for a collection of lodges in one locality or under one Assistant Provincial Grand Master for example. It would be appreciated if the reader could bear this in mind if his region adopts one of the other titular options, but this request seems preferable to using Province/District and Group/District/Division throughout the text. The relatively recent creation of the first Metropolitan Grand Lodge as the London equivalent of a Province, rather than remaining under the direct jurisdiction of the Grand Master, has also helped to avoid the requirement constantly to insert the London equivalent to Provincial protocol where appropriate. Where there are some specific differences between the operations of the District and Metropolitan Grand Lodges and the Provincial Grand Lodges, these are usually commented on as appropriate.

There are also some references to the Book of Constitutions (BoC), where appropriate paragraphs can explain in greater detail the different aspects of the Officer's duties and responsibilities, which may only have been alluded to in passing in this book. Where there are such references, the paragraph number is given as BoC114.

### Mentoring from the Candidate's Viewpoint

In these days of the internet and electronic libraries it is relatively easy to become educated in many aspects of life. So the new candidates for Masonry can gain an insight into Masonry from these sources, although it will only be a dispassionate assessment as they will not have experienced physical membership of a lodge.

For those who have researched and for those who have not, their first direct experience of Masonry will be at their initiation. Their involvement will be the exact opposite of our experience of a Russian doll. As you know, like peeling an onion, you open a doll to find another smaller one inside, and within that is another still smaller, etc. The first experience of the new candidate, however, is almost the reverse because his first contact with Masonry is with his lodge, which is equivalent to an inner doll. He then becomes aware of other lodges in the same area where he lives, probably within the same Group and Province (i.e. a larger doll). Thereafter he becomes aware of the United Grand Lodge of England, and then the family of Grand Lodges around the world (still larger dolls).

From another viewpoint, having read several pieces of Provincial and lodge mentoring literature, a common theme is that the three degrees in Craft Freemasonry represent birth, life and death. There can be little doubt that the birth of the candidate's formal career in Masonry has to be his first meeting; in this sense the previous social events and the lodge interview are interactions prior to joining. With the Fellowcraft degree again there is little doubt that a broadening of experience is being unfolded – after all, as the candidate you are told that 'you are now permitted to extend your researches into the hidden mysteries of Nature and Science.' In California they explain that the first degree is concerned with all things physical, while the second is concerned more with – as indeed is said in English ritual – 'the intellectual faculty'.

But I wonder if there needs to be some care with simply linking the third degree with death. Masonry is at pains to emphasise that it offers no route to salvation, nor immortality, nor is it an alternative to religion. Perhaps the key words are to be found halfway through the third degree, when the candidate is told to '… contemplate your inevitable destiny.' In this sense the question being posed to the candidate is not whether or not he will die, because he will at some time, but what does he want to achieve while he is still alive? How does he want to be remembered? There is almost a prelude to this consideration in the second degree working tools, where it is stated '… as the time will come, and the wisest of us knows not how soon, when … death, the grand leveller …'

In a way Freemasonry was centuries ahead of some BBC Horizon programmes in the early 1970's. Horizon compiled a trilogy of special programmes, entitled in the order of screening as 'the restless earth', 'the violent universe', and 'the inner world.' The first programme was concerned with our immediate surroundings, plate tectonics in moving the land masses around, and the power of terrestrial nature with earthquakes, volcanic eruptions, floods, glaciation, etc. The second programme looked around the universe (or as Carl Sagan would say, the cosmos), with novae and supernovae, the agglomeration of matter into planets and stars, black holes, and the effects of comets and asteroids colliding with planets. The last programme concerned itself with the complexities found inside man and the workings of the body and its organs, etc.

So the Horizon programmes covered first our immediate surroundings (an intermediate-size Russian doll), then the rest of the worlds surrounding us in an exploratory or investigative way (larger dolls), and finally looked inwards on ourselves in a reflective and contemplative way (smallest doll). Perhaps the three Masonic degrees mirror the concept of those three television programmes more closely than a simple birth, life and death cycle.

### Characteristics of a Mentor

It should be said at the outset that almost anyone can be a mentor, just as almost any man can be a father. And there are some similarities between the two roles. The father will try to gently guide his children through their first steps in life and in the world, and the mentor will do the same for a newcomer in Masonry. And the father and the mentor have a common attribute: they both have more experience than their child or charge – one with experience in life, the other in Freemasonry, and they want to pass on the benefit of that experience as efficiently as possible.

How much experience is necessary to perform the job well is an interesting question. It is very useful to have a wide-ranging knowledge of all things Masonic, so that every question posed can be answered with authority. And then I recall an exam question I once encountered: 'To be competent at your job, is it necessary to have all of the job knowledge in your head, or knowing where to find it when necessary? Discuss.' In other words, how should one organise knowledge? Does one clutter one's head with all sorts of tables of facts and figures, or should one have access to almanacs and other literature where you can quickly look up what you want? The latter may be useful even if you have learned a table of figures, as many people will sometimes want to check their memory – especially as they grow older. Thus the mentor does not need to have encyclopaedic knowledge, but he should have a range of contacts that between them can answer almost every question of the newcomer.

For some, the lodge mentor should be one of the father figures of the lodge, who has seen the lodge operating in the old days, knows why many of the lodge traditions have evolved, knows plenty about Provincial and Grand Lodge operations, etc. He would be able to, from his wide experience and many years in the Craft, directly answer the vast majority of questions that will be posed to him. For others a relative Masonic youngster, who has just gone down the road of discovery about things Masonic himself, would be the ideal mentor, because he can relate from his own recent experience how he approached finding out more about the organisation he had just joined and wanted to enjoy to the full. While he may not know as much as the more experienced Mason, he can pass on the useful sources of information that he has discovered and that the newcomer can investigate personally. And he has the ability to pull in any other lodge member, including the father figure, as required to answer any question from his greater experience or discuss matters more thoroughly than the younger mentor can himself.

But old or young Masonically, the mentor must also be someone who has people skills and can communicate with the newcomer. This is sometimes made easier if there is some common ground between the mentor and newcomer, perhaps working in the same line of business, having attended the same school or college, following the same sport or supporting the same team, etc. From this mutual interest a relationship can be struck up that will make the mentor's job significantly easier to perform.

The mentor must also be a good listener. He has to be able to understand the problems or questions of the newcomer, otherwise he will be using a scattergun approach of trying to answer everything in the hope that some aspects of his answers hit the target. There is an excellent quotation: 'I find that I learn nothing when my mouth is engaged.' Being a good communicator is not just talking endlessly. Let the newcomer try to enunciate his requests for information, and then you can target them accurately. And if in the dialogue you can help him to define his questions, then the chances are that you will be touching on other fringe issues which, by being close to the target area, are also helpful to his gaining a better understanding of Masonry.

The mentor must be capable of wearing many hats, including that of being a teacher, one who can inspire people to want to learn more, and one who enables them to assimilate learning into their lifestyle. There is also a coaching aspect (and in the USA the term coach is often used for this mentor role), and coaches encourage their students to build on their strengths, educate them how to tackle areas where improvement is needed, and enable them to have continued and increased enjoyment and success in Masonry. And there is the advisory role, so you should be regarded by the candidate as someone who could be a role model for him to emulate, and one who has credibility in and knowledge of Masonry, but who is not afraid of calling someone else if more detailed knowledge is required.

The mentor should have an enthusiasm for many aspects of Masonry, and have a generally relaxed and encouraging approach. He should have the ability to suggest and consider other options if the first route forward appears to be impracticable, and also be open to changes of circumstances and even criticism. A bonus would be to have the patience to see things through in the long term, and being quietly persuasive rather than in any way dictatorial, even if he knows by experience that the problem has only one solution which is obvious to him. And perhaps of most importance, he needs the new Mason to be sure that anything that is said will be treated in strict confidence rather than made public to a wider audience (this is the fourth point of fellowship in action) – often only by two people being totally open and candid can the real problems be stated and then addressed.

The mentor must also recognise the varying capabilities of the newcomers. Not all will be superb ritualists and efficient organisers, but will bring a variety of talents into the lodge. Some will be put off by an insistence that mastery of the ritual is a pre-requisite for advancement, although with time and encouragement they could surprise themselves with what they can accomplish, so they will need time to settle into the Craft. Also the mentor must be able to recognise family or work commitments that may limit the time available for lodge activities. There is no harm in declaring a time out for a member who has to concentrate on these aspects of his life – I have often said to lodge newcomers that there is no doubt that family come first, work comes second, and Masonry will fit in and around these where it can. If you don't agree that family comes first, would you stay at work if you were told that your wife or child had been involved in a traffic accident and rushed to hospital? And hopefully your work colleagues would agree. So if a member needs to sit on the lodge back benches for a while, let him do so. And then when his time frees up a little, be there to support him if he considers starting on the ladder of progression to the Master's chair.

The mentor also has to have the time himself to be able to perform this duty. There is little point in being very attentive to the newcomer's needs for a few weeks, and then leaving him to his own devices thereafter. This is not necessarily saying that the mentoring is a cradle to grave responsibility, but one can see it lasting from the initiation until the newcomer has been Master of the lodge, for example. Once out of the Chair, the Past Master has been in probably every junior office in the lodge and done everything that is included therein, and should himself have some experience in most matters Masonic. However, it is not just a question of attending every lodge meeting with the newcomer. It is having the time to be available on the phone, to exchange e-mails, or to hold an informal meeting whenever the newcomer seeks advice or clarification. It may also include having the time to take him to another lodge to see a ceremony he has just gone through himself, or to hear a lecture or see a demonstration that will enhance his knowledge and enjoyment of Masonry.

In this respect you should not be afraid of involving someone else in the process. As the newcomer finds his feet in the lodge and in Masonry, he will form natural relationships and liaisons with other members of the lodge. If the lodge mentor has the task of overseeing the development of all newcomers, then in a busy lodge with a lot of initiates he will become rapidly overwhelmed. So to pass on the individual reins to another member of the lodge may be a natural progression that should occur in many cases. The system advocated by many Provinces is that each newcomer has an individual mentor assigned to him, with a lodge mentor co-ordinating them. The co-ordination aspect may be useful if a visit is arranged to a neighbouring lodge for a special event, or to a Masonic museum, etc., when several newcomers and mentors may travel together.

In fact some Provinces prefer the term 'mentor co-ordinator' instead of lodge mentor, and recommend the use of individual mentors for each new Mason, and this is also the way mentoring or coaching is organised widely in the USA. In some US jurisdictions there it is specifically stated that the individual mentor or coach is to be a Master Mason, so he will be someone of a junior status. In a way this highlights what is said to a Master Mason when he receives his apron, that the new badge indicates that he is expected to offer assistance and instruction to those yet to attain that status – what better way to do so than to make him personally responsible for helping a new member as soon as that person has joined?

In many Grand Lodges in the USA, a Mason has to 'pass off' the degree he has just gone through before he is considered ready to go through the next, so there is very little of going through 3 degrees in 3 successive months. The 'passing off' is a question and answer session that can cover all aspects of the former degree, in front of a committee of other lodge members, and his mentor or coach will guide him through the preparation for this. In an era when English Masons are heard saying that the young men of today do not have the time to devote to learning Masonic ritual like they did in the old days, they should see the detail that this passing off entails – for example, in some jurisdictions one question is to repeat the obligation of the degree, and another to repeat the charge that was given. Not insignificant tasks, but there is immediately one significant benefit: when the newcomer occupies the Chair of the lodge, he has already learned all of the obligations (yes, they need to 'pass off' the third degree before they are allowed to join any side degrees). Rather than scaring away new Masons in the USA by expecting this level of comprehension of the ritual so early in a Masonic career, currently there appears to an increase in the number of candidates and a high level of retention of enthusiastic new Masons in several of the states. And in many instances, the new Mason and his coach become firm friends.

So if the same friendships should occur in an English lodge, the lodge mentor can take advantage of it and pass on the overseeing of the development and further coaching of the new Mason to a colleague. The latter can always discuss any aspects of his assumed responsibilities with the lodge mentor, and indeed with other individual coaches, so the lodge mentoring then becomes a team approach. This has another useful benefit, in that if any coach is taken ill or suddenly work or family commitments increase so that he cannot continue his coaching activities as fully as before, then another member of the team can step in and assist in an almost seamless manner. There should be no time in the new Mason's life that he feels alone – the lodge members should become an extended family for him, and families rally round whenever problems occur within it, with the adage that 'a problem shared is a problem halved.'

The lodge mentor should also be aware of what information and booklets are provided by Province or by his local Group. Many Provinces have such information, sometimes in the form of advice to mentors themselves, which you will want to share with any colleagues who are maintaining direct contact with the newcomer. Other Provinces have created a series of booklets that can be given to the new Mason after each degree, in some ways similar to the earlier Peterborough booklets. These booklets will answer some of the questions that the candidate may have, in trying to understand more fully the degree he has just been through, and may also serve to stimulate other questions or topics for discussion. Metropolitan Grand Lodge has a very detailed booklet to be given the new initiate, and it is worth obtaining a copy if your Province does not have such booklets. The details about the workings of Metropolitan Grand Lodge will not help the new Mason in a Province, but the rest of the general information is useful, and it may form the basis of a future Provincial booklet. Otherwise Provinces such as Somerset have made their booklets after each degree available for other Provinces to adapt and build on if they wish, and may also be worth obtaining if your Province does not already have its own booklets, but first check what is available from your Provincial mentor.

Some Provinces have booklets with lectures to be given in lodge, perhaps by the mentor, and designed to encourage the members question how the degree ceremonies are to be interpreted for example. There are also websites with additional information, of which the Provincial Mentor can inform you. Use as many sources of such information as you can, because they may cover aspects that are causing some underlying concern to the candidate but which he is not able to articulate clearly and thereby gain clarification. So just as the new Mason should not feel that he is left alone, neither should the lodge mentor feel that he is ploughing a lonely furrow – ask, share, combine, and you will find one of the sometimes almost intangible jewels of this order we are in – a truly supportive brotherhood.

The Provincial mentor may require updates and reports from each lodge mentor on every newcomer during the first few years of his Masonic career. This feedback can be invaluable, in possibly determining common problems cited by several new Masons, and which can be addressed at a Provincial level. It may also guide the Provincial mentor in what additional information would be beneficial to the lodge and individual mentors, so that he can arrange for it to be provided. And the Provincial mentor will doubtless be comparing notes with other Provinces, especially those adjacent to his own, and there may be occasions when some inter-Provincial collaboration such as joint seminars and meetings can benefit new members on a wider basis than being limited to those in the one Province. The data from the lodges will be useful to the Provincial mentor who may himself have to prepare a report for his Provincial Grand Master on the progress of all newcomers into the Province over the last year.

It would be useful if the lodge or individual mentor can gain positive feedback from the newcomer that he feels he is fitting into Masonry, and that Masonry is helping him become a better citizen. And this depends on the rapport built up between the newcomer and his individual and lodge mentors. If for any reason there is negative feedback, try to ascertain the causes, and then try to address them. Not every mentor-newcomer partnership will succeed in the long term, and as stated before the newcomer is aware that he has joined a Masonic family. So as he proceeds, it may be that another lodge member will find a greater empathy with him, and another relationship is started – perhaps one that will see him through the next stages of his development. So while some partnerships do become lifelong friendships, not every one will – people change with time, just as the teenager who goes to university often comes back with a new outlook and set of ideals than when he started his degree course. There should be a large enough range of capabilities of members within most lodges to accommodate such developments. And the mentoring cascade offers support in all aspects of the job – upwards, downwards and sideways, so take advantage of it if and when the need arises.

A short time ago the Provincial Grand Masters' Forum requested that a group of people review where the concept of mentoring was in different Provinces, and try to pull together best practices for the benefit of others, as some Provinces have adopted the concept and others are for the while still assessing it. There was a presentation by the group in Grand Lodge in 2008, and currently there is a forum of promoters of mentoring who are exchanging ideas, information and best practice with one another. The whole concept is developing and evolving, and will continue to do so for some time to come. Doubtless some of the early ideas will be modified in the light of better concepts, and some will be discarded altogether, and the Provinces which are late starters will have the benefit of that optimisation process. The question then has to be raised, whether or not one waits for the completion of the whole process, or begins to implement some of the key and useful elements now and accept that there will be some evolution of the process in time.

This book has been written to be of use to those who want to learn more about the general responsibilities and requirements in the role of being a mentor, or about applying some of the aspects of mentoring to the benefit of the lodge in the interim. It is meant to be complimentary to the effort being expended elsewhere, and not an assessment of what that process has so far achieved or might achieve in time. The next chapters cover some of the items you as a mentor might want to bear in mind at almost every stage of the newcomer's development in Masonry.

# The Candidate for Initiation

The first question posed to a candidate about to be passed to the second degree is:

'Where were you first prepared to be made a Mason?'

'In my heart.'

This means that Masonry accepts that people coming into the Craft for the first time are in a sense not made Masons on their first night, but are the type of people who are already acting in the manner befitting Masons. Masonry then gives them another framework or perspective by which to guide and shape their future lives and conduct, emphasising aspects that may have been latent before.

Thus some aspects of the mentoring of a newcomer should begin before he becomes a member of the Craft. How often do you hear the comment that someone has come into Freemasonry, but it wasn't for him? Should that candidate not have been fully aware of what he was getting himself into, before he committed himself to Masonry?

There are three essential areas in which candidates are expected to comply, and they are:

Spiritual – having a belief in a Supreme Being; Masonry is not a religion, but does require that each member acknowledges an omnipotent being;

Moral – being of good reputation and obedient to the laws of the land, not having a criminal record, being a good citizen in your locality, and loyal to your country;

Physical – being male and at least 21 years old (the age bar is lowered to 18 years in certain circumstances, BoC157).

Grand Lodge has published two booklets for people enquiring about Freemasonry. In the first, *'Freemasonry: An Approach to Life'*, it is clearly stated that the Craft is open to men of all faiths, who are law-abiding, of good character, and have a belief in God. It is a multi-cultural and multi-racial organisation, offering fraternal friendship to all men of goodwill and who have open minds. It is not a political organisation, and indeed requires that there is no discussion of religion or politics at its meetings. Whilst sometimes viewed as a secret society, it is open about what it does, raising and donating a large amount of money every year to charities, Masonic and non-Masonic, and its meeting places are well known within the local communities and can often be hired for use by the public if required.

In the booklet *'Your Questions Answered'*, the aspect of secrecy is addressed, and it is noted that much of our activities are already in the public domain, but we reserve the right to have private meetings for members only, as do many other organisations. No-one should join Freemasonry with a view to profiting from his contacts, and there are penalties for so doing which could lead to expulsion. Neither do Masons only look after themselves; while there are charitable funds established to help Masons in need – possibly assistance in old age, or when requiring medical treatment, Grand Lodge regularly makes donations every year to non-Masonic charities and to disaster relief agencies around the world – Masons look outwards as well as inwards. And the reason for adopting terms like the Volume of the Sacred Law and the Great Architect is so that men of all faiths can agree on wording that is neutral with regard to their individual beliefs, rather than slanted towards one religion or another.

For many lodge members, the interaction with the newcomer starts with the lodge committee interview. But in most cases for the proposer and seconder the process should have started several weeks and months, even years, beforehand. And the mentor should liaise with them to ensure that the potential candidate has all the information he needs to make a serious and considered decision on whether or not to join the lodge and Freemasonry. There may be Provincial booklets introducing Freemasonry to those interested in joining, so make sure that you have copies to give to the proposer and seconder for them to pass on to their potential candidates. Additionally there may be information on the Provincial website as well as the Grand Lodge website of interest to non-Masons, and they can give him the website addresses.

His additional introduction to Freemasonry can take several forms, depending on how your lodge operates. If you have several social functions (dinner-dances, barbecues, bowling days, white table lodge meetings) every year, then invite the prospective candidates and their ladies along, and let them assess for themselves what <u>they</u> are getting themselves into. Do not underestimate the role of the lady in this; if she does not support her man and his Masonic endeavours, there is nothing surer than he will leave the lodge after a time – Masonry does not and should not split families. In fact, depending on the age of the prospective Mason and his family, it may be advisable to check that he has full family support for his new venture. If there are already Masons in the family, then there should be no problems, and indeed the newcomer should be aware of what Masonry entails from those family members, if they are still alive.

Through such lodge events, the newcomer may have already met several lodge members socially. One benefit from this is that when it comes to the lodge committee interview, he should know and recognise several faces around the room. Not that all of the lodge needs to be involved in the interviewing process. Many lodges use up to five members – the proposer and seconder, the Master, the Secretary, and another, perhaps the Almoner or possibly now the lodge mentor. Before the interview, the mentor should check with the proposer and seconder that they have covered all of the preliminary information that should be given to a candidate. If not, then at the meeting the mentor can cover the ground for them. The reason for this is becoming more apparent in recent years; while some lodges are attracting new members, a proportion of them do not stay, and part of the reason for this may be that the newcomer was expecting something different in Masonry that he is disappointed not to have found.

Do not underplay the amount of time that Masonry will take up. If the lodge meets eight times each year, then there may be two practice meetings for each lodge meeting – perhaps one for juniors in the lodge and the other a full rehearsal of the coming lodge meeting coupled with a lodge committee meeting. Thus already for almost half of the weeks in the year the lodge is expecting the member to attend, and then there are the lodge socials, ladies evenings, visiting other lodges, possibly additional Group activities, new Masons' dinners, and other celebrations. And this is before the member begins to explore the possibilities of joining some of the Masonic degrees beyond the Craft – Masonry can quickly and literally take over a person's life, and he may not be ready for this to happen, and perhaps his family is not ready for this commitment.

There are also the significant costs of being a Mason, not only lodge dues and regalia, but the almost ever-present calls on a person's charitable instincts. In many Provinces, where they take the fundraising during a Festival very seriously, there is the possibility of stretching a member's purse a little too far by repeated requests for digging deeper into one's pockets. The final decision should always be between the person and his conscience, but there can be a lot of pressure applied which may at times be overdone. Reminders yes; arm-twisting all the way up the back perhaps not.

There is no need to frighten a potential Mason away, and it can be diplomatically explained that Masonry can probably expand to fill every minute of your spare time if that is what he wants, but he can always start lower down on the ladder of attendance and take more on when he is comfortable in doing so.

Assuming that the interview process is successful, each prospective candidate should be aware that after the interview his application to join the lodge and Freemasonry will be put formally to the lodge for a secret ballot by all of the members. His application form will have been scrutinised prior to that, and if the ballot proves successful, then the Secretary will send a letter of confirmation, and indicating on what date his initiation is planned to take place, at what time he should arrive at the hall, and what he should wear. Obviously the proposer or seconder can go through any other questions that the candidate may have, and may also co-ordinate their travel arrangements together.

# The Member after Initiation

## Introduction

The newcomer to Masonry, after his initiation night, may or may not be full of questions about the ceremony he has just gone through. Some will have good memory retention, and will ask their proposer or seconder or mentor why this was done, why that was said, who was doing what, and he may even want to be instructed in the layout of the lodge. Other initiates will want to think over what they have just experienced, and will be happy to think about the flashbacks that they can remember over a period of time.

So at the festive board, when he is probably sitting with his proposer and seconder, do not necessarily pound him with questions such as what did you think of that, did he understand the whole obligation, did he understand the symbolism of his preparation, etc. Take your lead from him. For some, who have been concentrating hard on repeating what they are told to say and following the many instructions of the Junior Deacon, just familiarising himself with the method of starting his response to the toast to his health and long membership of the lodge will be enough. He is the only one at the festive board for whom this protocol is brand new, and most initiates want to open their short speech of acknowledgement as competently as they can, to reflect positively on their proposers and seconders.

But how might the mentor prepare himself for the questions that will, sooner or later, come from the initiate? He may want to mull over what has happened to him, and then ask questions from time to time in the weeks leading up to his next meeting. You may have arranged to meet up with him again, before his next ceremony, in order to go through the questions and answers he has been asked to learn. One way of structuring your possible replies is to go through the initiation ceremony as he did, by splitting the ceremony and the evening into their component parts: the initial presentation, the obligation, the demonstration, and the explanation.

## Recalling the Degree Ceremony
### Presentation

Hopefully the proposer and/or the seconder will have been able to bring the candidate to his first lodge meeting. Having a friend by his side is a enormous boost to his confidence when stepping into the unknown. Without spoiling his experience on the night, the candidate can be told some of the general arrangements of the Masonic meetings – the formal opening of the lodge, the introduction of the candidate to the lodge, the conducting of a traditional ceremony, the routine business of the lodge for the members, and the meal afterwards.

After the candidate's arrival at the Masonic hall before the lodge meeting, it is useful for the lodge Officers to introduce themselves to him, and possibly briefly to say what their role will be on the night: the Tyler will be preparing him for the ceremony; the Deacons will be escorting him round; the Wardens will be asking him a few questions – for which the Deacons will prompt his replies; and the Master will be guiding him through a somewhat lengthy commitment to Masonry are some examples. The proposer or seconder can make the introductions, or possibly the mentor can step in at this stage and perform this duty. Either way the candidate will be put at ease if he has at least spoken to some of the participants in the ceremony before the meeting itself. And possibly the most important of these will be the Junior Deacon, who will be personally escorting him, and the Master, who will be interacting with him throughout the ceremony.

The candidate is then probably left alone as all of the lodge members and visitors disappear into a closed room. During the opening of the lodge, he will probably be requested to sit in another room, rather than to distract the Tyler from his duties outside the door of the lodge. This will especially be so if it is the lodge tradition to formally process into the lodge room, although some lodges will not mind the candidate seeing their Masonic regalia prior to the meeting. After all, there have been public processions of Masons in the past, and there was a video of Grand Lodge parading into the main lodge room at Great Queen Street, so a knowledge of how Masons appear in formal dress is already in the public domain, if the candidate has researched Masonry at all.

However, it would be appropriate for someone, possibly the mentor, to stay with the candidate rather than leave him totally alone before his initiation. It would not be difficult for the mentor to slip back into lodge after the candidate has entered. It may be worth trying out the concept, and then gaining feedback from the next few candidates if this helped to calm their nerves, etc. And if the proposer has intimated that his candidate has a naturally nervous disposition, then it might be entirely appropriate in this instance, rather than leave him to his own devices. There are stories about candidates disappearing through the lavatory window rather than face an unknown lodge, and to have a candidate stressed to this extent may be taking the surprise element too far.

The Tyler can be very helpful in talking to the candidate while preparing him, perhaps explaining why he is making him take on a rather strange appearance. The candidate will normally be apprehensive of what he has let himself in for, and wondering what exactly happens behind those closed doors with their sonorous knocks. If the Tyler can allay some of his worst fears, with a few words or a wink, then the candidate will enter the lodge with a greater degree of confidence while at the same time trying to look calm on the exterior despite what thoughts might be racing through his mind at this time. If the Tyler or the mentor can think back to when he himself was initiated, then there is nothing wrong with comparing his own feelings and thoughts with those of the candidate while they are waiting for the door to be opened by the Inner Guard and the first questions of the degree to be asked.

The preparation of the candidate begins by him taking off some of his clothes and removing all of his valuables – the latter being an undoubted step of faith, so there will already be some apprehension rising in his mind. But this is nothing compared to when the blindfold is placed about his head, and he has thereafter to rely on gentle shepherding by others to guide him on his way to the next part of the ceremony. Most Tylers slip on the cable tow after blindfolding, as this prevents too many questions. I recall that at my initiation I had seen some visitors going into lodge after the formal opening while I was being prepared. Having noted that they were wearing collars, I was blindfolded, and then assumed when I felt something placed about my neck that I was also being collared, and it was quite a surprise when the cable tow was lifted from my shoulders after the obligation.

It may be the tradition in a lodge for the Secretary and Treasurer to leave the lodge room immediately before the ceremony, in order for the candidate to sign the declaration book as a new member, and to collect a cheque to cover his first year's subscription and joining fee (or these items may have been covered earlier in the evening). They will then return to the lodge room to report that all of the preliminary business has been transacted satisfactorily.

The candidate's entrance into the lodge is via a dialogue between the Tyler and the Inner Guard, the former responding on behalf of the candidate. The first words of the Tyler, being '… recommended, proposed and approved …', are merely summarising the mechanics of a new membership being discussed and agreed upon. His next words, '…, by the help of God, being free and of good report', are much more significant. One of the first questions at the lodge interview was to elicit confirmation of a belief in a Supreme Being, and without this the interview and the membership process has to be terminated. So on the candidate's first entry into lodge, this belief is re-emphasised. He also has to be free to request membership for himself, and he needs to be of good character – later on he will be reminded that if he proposes anyone else into Masonry he should ensure that the newcomer has a similarly good character reference. In this sense the word 'free' can also refer to not being a slave, or bound to any other person (such as the lord of the manor in the past), and therefore not able to commit himself to join Masonry as a free agent.

The Inner Guard prods him and asks if he feels anything, but being blindfolded the candidate does not see the Inner Guard lift up the poignard to confirm that the implement has been properly applied. The Junior Deacon then collects the candidate and takes him to the kneeling stool or cushion. The Master asks him to confirm he is a man and at least 21 years old, the traditional age of majority. In some lodges, especially university ones, it is common to initiate candidates that are only 18 years old, with a dispensation from the Provincial Grand Master to do so. Nowadays the age of 18 has become the age of majority, but Masonry retains its traditions. The comment about the man is interesting, and the candidate will learn that in the world there are female Masons and lodges with mixed sexes, but these are not recognised by our Grand Lodge as maintaining the ancient landmarks of the Order.

He is then invited to kneel for prayer, an incantation that he will be guided in the future by the wisdom of God and the ways of Masonry, to become a worthwhile Mason. He is then challenged to declare in whom he places his trust to see him through any danger, and this time the Junior Deacon prompts him to repeat the Tyler's previous response on the candidate's behalf, 'In God.' There can be little doubt as to the importance placed on this basic belief at the heart of Masonry.

He is then led around the lodge room, being told to start walking with his left foot, and is challenged in turn by the Junior and Senior Wardens. The Junior Deacon introduces him each time, and again includes in his dialogues the reliance on a Supreme Being. The Senior Warden formally presents the candidate to the Master, who then puts three questions to the candidate, concerning his reasons for joining Freemasonry and an assurance that he will adhere to the Craft regulations.

The Master then requests that the candidate approaches the east by the proper steps or in due form. Although not explained now, the explanation of the proper steps is contained in some forms of the Craft ritual. The Master then assures the candidate that Masonry will not conflict with his religious beliefs or his duties as a citizen, and invites him to enter into an obligation concerning his Masonic responsibilities.

## Obligation and Demonstration

The first degree obligation is quite long, and includes a sentence that is 20 lines in length in the pocket ritual book, so is not necessarily easy for the candidate to fully comprehend it at the first hearing. But essentially it emphasises the need to keep Masonic secrets within Masonry, and it is expected that the candidate will behave honourably and abide by the rules of the Craft. The candidate may be interested to learn that the basic obligation has changed little from the first half of the 18th century, so participating in the initiation ceremony is stepping a long way into the past.

If the candidate is the son of the Master, as sometimes happens, there is an additional address from father to son on the latter's initiation. Whilst it tends to add to the emotions of the evening for the Master, it is a very personal part of a memorable family evening, and well worth the effort to deliver it properly – the sincerity will undoubtedly be there in the circumstances.

After removing the blindfold, some of the most important symbols in Masonry are shown to the initiate, and the senior lodge Officers are pointed out in their respective stations. The poignard and cable tow are shown to the candidate, and he is reminded of the traditional and symbolic penalty for not keeping his Masonic word. Then the secrets of an Entered Apprentice are taught to the initiate – the sign, grip and word, and he is despatched to the Wardens in order to demonstrate his new-found knowledge to both them and the lodge. However, rather than test the initiate's short-term memory at this juncture, the Junior Deacon steps in to prompt him with all of the required answers. At the same time the repeated actions and words are being taken in and learned by the initiate, so that very soon the reaction will be automatic when required in the future. And with the Senior Warden, the full answers cover some of the history of the different aspects of what he is doing.

The Senior Warden is then requested to invest the initiate with the badge of an Entered Apprentice, and some of the symbolism of the apron is explained. It is particularly notable that the plain apron forms the basis for all of the aprons of more senior Masons, emphasising the basic equality of all Masons whilst enjoying a whole range of Masonic ranks. There are several different versions of the apron address, and each has its own merits, although personally I enjoy the more detailed explanations as they try to inform the initiate as fully as possible of an interpretation of the symbolism.

There then follows the north east corner address, which emphasises the constant awareness of charitable giving which has been a characteristic of Masonry since the very early days. In fact several of the older lodges began life as friendly societies which offered self-help within the membership whenever the need arose. And such assistance was necessary in those days, before the National Health Service and unemployment benefit, because when someone was sick or out of work there would have been no money coming in to feed his family. This address many would say is the highlight of the degree, perhaps along with the charge, and if someone who knows the initiate is able to deliver it, then it will have added sincerity. And it has an increased poignancy if the collection for charity takes place during the address, as happens in some lodges – it makes for a moment in the ceremony that will be etched onto the initiate's memory for a long time afterwards. And the collection for charity also emphasises the fact that this is another part of the demonstration aspects of the ceremony – the candidate is asked to confirm personally what he has just said he would do, if he had the means to do so. The collection also serves to make the enunciation of the reasons for this test afterwards the more memorable – the north east corner really is a beautifully crafted piece of ritual.

## Explanation

After the comments about charity, the remainder of the ceremony is a series of explanations about different aspects of the ceremony. The next item is an explanation of the working tools of the degree, which are three in number and would have been used by the practising masons in their initial sizing and rough cutting of the stones for various uses. The symbolism of the 24 hours of the day is fairly straightforward; that of conscience being powerful enough to resist unworthy thoughts is also intelligible; but education is an interesting interpretation of the cutting implement. In Scotland the explanation of the third tool includes the comment that, although a diminutive instrument, it concentrates the force of the hammer to make even the hardest of stones yield to its repeated demands. And it perhaps emphasises that the initiate is now, on his first night in Masonry, at the start of a journey that encompasses increased knowledge and further education. And any Provincial mentor present may mentally finger his office jewel while the explanation is being made.

There then follows, normally after the candidate has been allowed to adjust his clothing to a more conventional appearance, another of the highlights of the degree, the charge after initiation. In some lodges the initiate will have been given a copy of the first degree charge, which he may be told is one of the few pieces of Masonic ritual that can be shown his family, or it may be in a booklet he will receive afterwards. The idea is that the family, and particularly his wife, who may be somewhat concerned of what exactly the man of the house has become a member, will have their fears at least partially allayed by reading the content of the charge. It lays out what the Craft expects of every member, and how it expects him to behave. In particular they may be relieved to learn that it is not in any way transcending his religious beliefs, his family responsibilities, or his respect for and adherence to the laws of the State. Hopefully they will see that Masonry encourages a man to become a better citizen of the world, and not to lose sight of his responsibilities to his fellow men, particularly when they need relief to which he can contribute in a responsible way.

The words at the end of the charge regarding a Mason are 'Virtue, Mercy and Honour', but these are translated in the questions and answers before the second degree as 'Brotherly Love, Relief and Truth', the Grand Principles of the Order. The first indicates that Masons are to show tolerance and respect for the opinions of others and behave with kindness and understanding; the second that there is a duty of care for others, within the lodge and outside; and the third that Masons should live by high moral standards and be truthful and honest in all of their dealings, and also encourage others to do likewise.

There are also three items of ritual that your lodge may or may not include. At the back of the book on Emulation ritual there is an explanation of the first degree tracing board. If you read it, you will understand that it is a very useful explanation of the lodge room and what its furniture and jewels represent. At the presentation of a Grand Lodge Certificate, it is said to the recipient that the design of the certificate is in some ways a guide to the lodge room. The formal explanation of the tracing board goes into much more detail, and covers many more aspects of the lodge room. If someone in your lodge does not already deliver this explanation to initiates, then you might suggest that one or a group of members learn it so that it can be delivered, either after the ceremony, or on another night when the initiate can sit in the lodge room in a somewhat more relaxed frame of mind than on his initiation night, and be able to absorb much more of the explanation. And there is additionally an introduction to the standard explanation, which covers a brief history of early Masonry and the development of tracing boards, and which helps to put into context what is to follow.

In some lodges there are also formal explanations of why the candidate was prepared the way he was, and these can also be delivered in lodge. The form of the preparation would have seemed somewhat unusual to him, and if you think back to your own initiation, then similar perplexity must have crossed your mind as well. Many lodges half-undress the candidate, adjusting different items of his clothing, while some go to the extent of having a change of clothing for him to put on. But unless you have an experienced Tyler outside the door of the lodge, who can not only put the candidate at ease while he is with him, but also go some way to explaining why he is being prepared in this manner, then these questions will remain in the initiate's mind until he raises them with you as mentor or with another lodge member. Again, if no-one in the lodge has delivered this item of ritual before, you might consider arranging for someone – perhaps even you as a mentor, to learn the explanation and to deliver it to the initiate at the end of the ceremony.

In some of the older lodges it was traditional for a new Mason to be presented with a pair of white gloves, as another emblem of purity. The wearing of white gloves in lodges is surprisingly not mandatory, and the lodge can decide that members should or should not wear them; Grand Lodge recommends that whichever way the decision is made, then all present should conform. The white gloves were usually donated by the initiate's proposer and seconder, and sometimes a second pair were given for lady of the initiate to wear. There is a short address explaining the history of the tradition, and ensures that the candidate is properly clothed in his first meeting – if the lodge has chosen to wear gloves. But also note that some lodges only expect a candidate to begin to wear white gloves after he has been made a Master Mason, so the formal presentation can be delayed until then.

Even if you decide as a lodge not to perform these additional parts of ritual in the lodge, then you as lodge mentor, and perhaps also the proposer or seconder, should obtain copies of them, as they will provide a useful resource when answering the initiate's questions. And if your lodge has several juniors who are Stewards or just sitting on the sidelines during ceremonies, then to have a group of them learn these parts of ritual will not only give them a chance of performing on the lodge room floor, but will also educate them as they read and learn the different parts, and they will be able to answer the questions of future candidates more proficiently themselves.

Finally in some lodges the questions and answers, which the candidate will have to learn and deliver at the start of the second degree, are enunciated by the members of the lodge. This may include the Master, the Wardens, or other members, but it is particularly appropriate that, after hearing so much memorised ritual during his initiation, the candidate is immediately thrown into this activity by giving him something to learn. They are a shorthand version of some aspects of the first degree, and in the early lodges the minutes reveal that the next ceremony was sometimes postponed if on the night the candidate proved incapable of having committed to memory even these first and relatively simple steps in remembering the ritual. These days a Deacon will prompt him if necessary, but it would be better for the candidate if he can successfully deliver his eleven answers without assistance, as he will feel he has achieved something in the early days of his Masonic career.

Finally in the ceremony the candidate was handed a Book of Constitutions and the bylaws of his lodge. Some candidates will glance through the lodge bylaws afterwards, but it would be surprising if they all sat down and went through the Book of Constitutions after the meeting. Indeed I imagine that many have gone through the chair of the lodge without reading it, preferring to rely on the Secretary or Director of Ceremonies to advise the Master as necessary. The 300-plus pages in the book will not mean very much to a new Mason, but the pictures of the aprons and office jewels will help him to identify the Provincial ranks and the lodge Officers, once he is aware of the different symbols. And perhaps the Master Elect should be reminded to look at the paragraphs covering the workings of a private lodge and his duties as Master (BoC94-191) before his year commences.

Whilst on the subject of books and printed information, some Provinces in their booklet for initiates have copied out the full charge and sometimes the explanation of the working tools, as well as the questions and answers leading to the second degree, and added some useful background material as an introduction to Masonry. This can contain a lot of information about the degree, and explain many aspects of the ceremony and the layout of the lodge room, and will help the initiate to understand more of the symbolism which, without guidance, may not be immediately apparent. Some make the point that the charge is perhaps a rather long way of describing their expectations of the candidate's future behaviour, and in summary it requests him to:

- be honourable in all of his dealings, with Masons or non-Masons;
- be a good and helpful neighbour;
- be attentive to his civic responsibilities and loyal to his country;
- cheerfully donate to charity what he can afford;
- obey the regulations of Masonry;

- attempt to learn more about the organisation he has just joined.

The booklets also serve as a reminder of what happened at his initiation and in some cases contain explanations of why various things were said and done, which serves as a useful aide-memoire for him.

## Aftermath

The initiate must feel at ease in the after-lodge activities prior to and including the festive board. He has to feel that he has joined a new family, where everyone welcomes him as the latest member and wishes him every success in the future. So it is appropriate for the Master and other Officers as well as members of the lodge to go out of their way to take the time to speak to him. That means that he will have a bewildering array of names and faces to try to remember, but the overall feeling will be one of acceptance. The alternative of being left almost alone with his proposer and seconder is not worth considering, but rather than leave it to one two members to speak to him, make sure that all of the members make the effort to do so. And this process can start in the lodge after the Master and dignitaries have processed out, if they do, when a quick handshake of welcome will suffice and will be appreciated. And while he is standing at the bar before the meal starts, then the remaining members should welcome him among them. Or after the meal, they may make a point of going up to him and perhaps congratulating him on his speech as well as welcoming him into the lodge and Masonry.

During the meal and before the formal toasts, the Master may request some brethren to take wine with him. All invited should stand and raise a glass in compliance with the request, and at an appropriate point this may include not only any dignitaries present but also the initiate and perhaps his proposer and seconder, so he should be warned about the eventuality.

It is worth noting that some lodges have a sung grace before and/or after the meal; may also sing an ode for absent brethren, traditionally at 9 o'clock, when the hands of the clock are at the square; and possibly a song to the visitors. If your lodge does any of these, then make sure that the initiate has a copy of what is being sung, so that he knows what is going on, and hopefully he can pick up the tunes quickly. It is always embarrassing, and you must have felt this when visiting another lodge and they strike up a song with which you are not familiar. And hopefully your lodge will have the opening and closing odes on printed sheets for members and visitors, as the initiate will have required the words of the latter at the end of his first lodge meeting. Attention to this kind of detail can confirm the caring nature of our organisation, that we take great pains to advocate. If the lodge sings an Entered Apprentice's song, then he is the subject of it and can relax and enjoy himself, although he will need the words of that song for the next candidate who becomes a member.

The lodge may also have the tradition of firing after toasts – banging the firing glasses on the tables and applauding. It is a simple rhythm to pick up, so should not take the candidate too long to join in, but it might again be worth warning him about it if you can.

Whether from reading any booklets given to him, or remembering aspects of his initiation, the new Mason may have some early questions which may involve purely domestic matters, such as how often are the fees paid, how do I book a meal, how do I bring a guest, do I wear the same clothing for all meetings, do I need to buy a white apron? These can be easily dealt with, and some lodges give the initiate an introductory letter from the Master, which sets out the calendar of events, practice meetings, socials, the summons and sending apologies when he cannot attend, and so on. If a list of members of the lodge and their addresses and telephone numbers can be given him at the same time, then he has the means to make contact if the need arises. Alternatively the lodge mentor can draft a similar letter, giving his own contact details and those of the individual mentor assigned to the newcomer.

At or after the first meeting, the initiate will probably have been given the questions and answers leading to the second degree. How long he will need to wait for this next ceremony will depend on the amount of work before the lodge and the number of candidates and new Masons en route to becoming Master Masons. There are some lodges which will not take one candidate through the next ceremony until another candidate has joined the lodge. The initiate therefore may have only 4 weeks until his next ceremony, or several months.

Either way, this short piece of ritual may be the first item of prose that he has had to commit to memory since being taught about poetry in school. But it is really not much different to learning a short speech that he wanted to deliver properly – to a colleague, to a friend, to his lady, or as the best man at a wedding, so there will have been many occasions when the content of what he wanted to say was important but not necessarily the exact words that he would use. This time the exact words are important, so the learning has to be more thorough. Another way of looking at it is that we have all grown up with songs, whether in our early years at school, singing hymns in church, or when we cannot stop some pop songs repeating themselves in our heads. In songs the words are important, otherwise the lines do not scan properly; in these Masonic questions and answers the use of incorrect words will cause a halt in the proceedings and some quick prompting from the Deacon.

It may be interesting to the initiate that in some of the older lodges they placed great importance on the candidate's ability to learn the answers properly – and it has been recorded in their minutes that they had deferred the ceremony if he could not show mastery of these few items. This may well be a throwback to the days when the ceremonies were short but were followed by formal lectures, sometimes delivered in a catechismal form. New members were expected to memorise the lectures and to participate in them for the benefit of later candidates, before they themselves were deemed fit to progress further in the Craft. In those early days of Freemasonry, when not everyone could read, committing the different aspects of each degree to memory was very important. The current requirement for 11 questions and answers to be memorised as an alternative does not seem to be an unreasonable one.

The questions and answers are effectively a shorthand version of some of the highlights of the first degree. If the initiate can remember these aspects, then he will be able to see what they are testing; if he does not remember them, then you can talk them through with him. In this sense the booklet, by summarising the ceremony, enables the initiate to picture what happened to him in his mind, and then the answers he has to learn will become more relevant to his own recent experience.

Why the emphasis on memorising the ritual? In some constitutions almost everything is read out of a book, but that can at times feel like a series of short formal lectures. By memorising a piece of ritual, its delivery creates more impact on the candidate, and it seems almost conversational and to flow much better than when read out. Additionally the candidate will find that, when he tries to learn any piece of ritual, no matter how many times he has already heard it beforehand, it can take on a new meaning – perhaps one that was not immediately obvious. In the learning process the sentences of the piece of ritual are broken down, analysed for how they should be spoken aloud, and recombined in a format that may be unique to the person going through the exercise. So be it; each Mason will bring his individual character into whatever he does. And sometimes when a member of another lodge is delivering a piece of ritual that you have done regularly yourself, and the emphasis or intonation is not quite the way you have adopted, suddenly another interpretation of the piece comes into your mind – some parts of our Masonic ritual make up a rich tapestry of meanings indeed.

It is useful if there is another candidate coming into the lodge soon afterwards. The previous initiate can now sit though the ceremony, not concentrating on repeating what he has been told to say, and standing and kneeling as appropriate, etc., and he can take in the entire ritual. Sometimes there will be flashbacks to his own initiation, and on other occasions he will be thinking did that happen in my own ceremony because it had not registered at all. If your lodge does not have another initiation lined up, then there may be another lodge nearby that does, and you have the chance of taking your new member along to see it. The other lodge may do things slightly differently from yours, so there may be completely new parts to the ceremony which your member did not go through, but the essentials will all be there.

If there are other new members of the lodge in front of this latest one, then the lodge may progress them through their second or third degrees before the newest recruit advances further. He will therefore be asked to retire from the lodge while work is performed in the higher degrees. While he is outside the lodge room, the Tyler may be able to discuss aspects of Masonry with him, or answer any questions he may have. However, the Tyler does have to attend to the candidate for the higher degree, in preparing him for the first part of the ceremony, and restoring him to a more normal appearance before the second part. Thus he will not be able to give the initiate outside the door his full attention, and indeed has to move him elsewhere when he is introducing the candidate for the degree ceremony back into the lodge.

Several lodges already depute someone to go outside the lodge room with those who are excluded, often a senior member. But this person could well be the lodge mentor or, if he is participating in the ceremony, someone else such as the person's proposer or seconder. Although the discussion cannot include any aspects of the higher degree, this should be a useful time to review either the first degree, or items of lodge business, or covering wider aspects in

Masonry. The Mason accompanying the initiate outside the lodge room will hopefully be aware of what other experience the initiate has obtained since becoming a member, but the conversation can obviously cover whatever topics he may want to bring up.

Some initiates will not venture far from their own lodge in the early days of being a member of the Craft, and their lodge will be their only window on Freemasonry. They will see several visitors coming to the meetings, sometimes quite senior in rank (especially to installations), but they themselves may not venture beyond the four walls of their lodge room. If there are other lodges meeting in the same building, then there may be a greater degree of inter-visiting on an informal or formal basis, the latter perhaps being once a year to each other's lodge, in which case it may not be too difficult for you as mentor to arrange a visit to another lodge accompanied by the new member. Different areas of the country operate in different ways. In some, a car full of Masons (not always the same ones) will travel on most nights of the week to neighbouring lodges; in other areas there is far less inter-visiting. In the former case it is easy to invite the new member to join the group and visit another lodge, and he will be able to broaden his Masonic experience while being in the company of his new lodge friends.

For the initiate who is perhaps too busy to cope with additional nights of visiting other lodges, and perhaps noting the differences in the way each lodge conducts its business and its ceremonies, then he will probably be interested in some explanation of what the officers do and other aspects of life in the lodge. Some ideas on topics to discuss are given in the appendix of this book.

# The Member after Passing

## Introduction

The next degree for the new member is that of being passed to a Fellowcraft. At first glance it is only a short degree, not having the impact of the first ceremony, nor the dramatic content of the third degree. And yet this degree is one of the most important in the Craft. Originally there were only two degrees; being made an Entered Apprentice, and then being elevated in status to a Fellow of the Craft. There was no other degree in Craft Freemasonry. If you have read the content of the installation ceremony, you will already have noted that the first part is conducted in the second degree. The third degree is then merely opened as a prelude to opening the board of Installed Masters. In the second degree it is noted that the Master Elect has to have served the office of Warden, but then it is stated that he has to be 'an experienced Craftsman to preside over them.' Shortly afterwards it added that he has to have been initiated, passed and raised, but the fact that installation stems from the second degree is a throwback to this earlier two-degree system. The third degree was only developed towards the middle of the 18th century.

Thus the second degree, though undoubtedly shorter than the other two, is traditionally as far as the new member would go until elected as Master Elect. As a Craftsman, he would have to earn the respect of the other lodge members, especially the senior ones, by demonstrating his capability of mastering all aspects of the roles he has been given up until this time. In traditional practical masonry, this would have involved covering all of the facets of shaping of blocks of masonry and their subsequent incorporation into the final structure. In free and accepted Masonry it will involve capably discharging all responsibilities with which he is entrusted, and this will include those parts of the Masonic ritual that he has been requested to deliver.

But before reaching the eminence of Master Elect, he has to go through the second degree. He has learned his questions and answers, in most cases the first piece of Masonic ritual he will have committed to memory, and which will stand him in good stead when he becomes Junior Deacon. He might also have known what to expect to some extent, based on his experience of the first degree. He has the added advantage of not being blindfolded, so that he can see what happens in the ceremony, especially if he has had the chance to witness another new candidate go through his initiation degree, whether in his own lodge or another.

## Recalling the Degree Ceremony
### Presentation

For this degree he started his presentation inside the lodge room, perhaps with the Junior Deacon standing beside him as he answered the questions. He was then given a pass or passing grip and word with which to re-enter the lodge. And then he is handed to the Tyler to make him ready for the coming ceremony. Then once again he stood outside the lodge room, prepared by the Tyler in almost a mirror image of how he was prepared for his initiation. And again the Tyler and Inner Guard combined together to announce his wish to enter the lodge, this time to become a Fellowcraft, although the Inner Guard will check that he has remembered the means of re-entry. Again a Deacon came to escort him around the lodge. In some lodges up until the obligation it is the Junior Deacon who escorts the candidate; in others it is the Senior Deacon who does so from the start of the degree ceremony.

This time there was a short prayer, and then the perambulations. Again he might have guessed there would be more parading around the lodge room, and again the Deacon will have prompted him with all of the required answers, although the first word he was asked to repeat may have come as a surprise, in that it was delivered in full and not in component form as he had previously been instructed to do. But he was in open lodge rather than alone with a stranger, and he had already given the correct proofs of entrance into the lodge to the Inner Guard, so it was legitimate to have stated the word in full. He will ultimately have given those proofs to the Senior Warden, before the latter presented him formally to the Master.

He then approached the east in an unusual way – if you think about the direction of travel he is directed to take. How many winding staircases wind their way anticlockwise in ascending? The answer is very few. In all fortified buildings, castles and strong houses, or even towers and spires of churches they almost invariably wind upwards in a clockwise direction. One reason cited for this direction is that the attacking troops would always be trying to ascend the building, and the vast majority of them would have been right-handed. Thus the central column would have hindered the attacking troops by limiting the swing of their swords, while the defending troops above would have the advantage of wielding their swords more freely and fully – and the building would have been designed from a defensive viewpoint by the occupant. It should be noted that the number of steps taken to the east, five, is two more than in the first degree, so there is a built-in progression in some aspects of the first two degrees.

### Obligation and Demonstration

Perhaps these thoughts will not have crossed the mind of the candidate, as once again he was concentrating on doing as he was told. Arriving in the east, he was informed there would be another obligation, but again he might have guessed there would be. This time it was much shorter in length, and was essentially promising that the secrets of the current degree should be kept from those who are not of this rank in Freemasonry, i.e. Entered Apprentices, as well from non-Masons. He was then informed that the implements on the Holy Book have been adjusted from their placement in the first degree, and confirmed that the rank of Fellowcraft is halfway through the trigradal (three degree) system of the Craft.

He was then entrusted with a more complex sign than in the first degree, interestingly in three parts (although the third part refers to the discharge of the sign), and it was explained to him how each part arose. Whereas the sign in the first degree was given one-handed, this degree required both hands. The first part of the sign alluded to a character in the Old Testament, which is perhaps a pointer that some of the future symbolism will be developed from the same source (as the tracing board will confirm). Also the part of the anatomy that was this time alluded to in the penal part of the signs is lower than that part referred to in the first degree, and again forms a logical progression to be completed in the third degree. Then he was once again escorted to the Wardens for them to check that he had taken on board what he has just been taught, although helpfully for those of a nervous disposition the Deacon again led a full and complete prompting session.

The Fellowcraft was then invested with a new apron, depicting his more elevated status in the Masonic hierarchy. The standard apron address from the Senior Warden was brief and to the point, but some lodges use a longer address that alludes to the representation of the ancient elements of fire and water, and which echo the words of the Master in stating that the Fellowcraft is at the midway of Masonry. The south east corner address reinforced this aspect, as in the first degree the equivalent address was made to the candidate standing in the north east – everything in the Masonic degrees emphasises that the candidate is on a journey of discovery.

Then came the important comment about the teaching of the second degree, when the candidate was informed that he is … 'now permitted to extend your researches into the hidden mysteries of Nature and Science.' And this is perhaps the key lesson of the degree. Whereas before the initiate concentrated on the immediate surroundings of the lodge and its members, and conducting himself personally within the principles of the Craft, he is now asked to widen his horizons outside those limits and embrace the wider aspects of Masonry and the world. He is now being asked to open a larger doll or two in the series of Russian dolls, and to operate on a larger stage than before. This wider horizon will include Provincial Grand Lodge and Grand Lodge itself, and several aspects of these two organisations are covered in the appendix of this book.

**Explanation**

Then immediately the candidate was brought back to the reality of the traditions of masonry, the working tools. These are all helping the craftsman to take the roughly prepared stone and to bring it to a finished and even perfect condition, and standing in the south east of the lodge the candidate may have had his feet about a perfect ashlar. The tools also enable the more skilled and experienced mason ('the more expert workman') to build structures vertically and horizontally, by placing the blocks of stone on top of and alongside one another in order to complete the edifice. Wasn't this also initially referred to in the north east address in the first degree?

In several lodges the long version of the explanation of the working tools, to be found at the back of the emulation ritual book, is used. If your lodge has traditionally performed the standard short version, then read through the long version and see if you as mentor or anyone else in the lodge wants to learn it as a variation. It is one of the best pieces of Craft ritual that exists. It emphasises that we are all created essentially as equals, although some will have risen to eminence among us, but also adds a comment about the level perhaps acting as a prelude to the third degree, by noting that we will all eventually die, '... and the wisest of us knows not how soon,' and that death will serve to reduce us all to the same level again – powerful stuff.

He might then have been given the explanation of the second

degree tracing board during the meeting, which when first heard by a candidate is an impressive testimony to a great deal of mental effort expended by the presenter to memorise it. Those who enjoy giving the explanation will often admit that, being a story, it is somewhat easier to learn than other parts of the Craft ritual. But nonetheless, if delivered with style it is something that has acted as an incentive for many new Masons to want to get to grips with learning the ritual in order to emulate that night when they first heard it in lodge. It is perhaps surprising that the first degree charge does not usually have the same effect, though that is an equally impressive slice of ritual to deliver. However, it was the candidate's first night in the Craft, and he has probably already been swamped with symbolism and somewhat drained by trying hard to concentrate on what was happening, and the charge is a collection of several disparate aspects of behaviour as a Mason; and there is no story line that efficiently links up the several themes of the charge.

The explanation of the tracing board is a separate story in its own right which, when thought about after the ceremony of passing, does not seem to have much direct relevance to what has happened beforehand. It does, however, lay the foundation for what is to come in the third degree, and also forms the basis for several side degrees if the new member chooses to widen his participation in Masonry at a later date. Much of our Masonic teaching is based on aspects of King Solomon's temple or, in the case of the Royal Arch, on Zerubabbel's temple which followed it.

The numbers three, five and seven are noted with respect to the winding staircase, referring to the three Master and his two Wardens, plus two Fellowcrafts, plus two Entered Apprentices. In England we note there were '… three, five, seven or more steps …' in the staircase in the temple; the three representing the Grand Masters Solomon of Israel, Hiram of Tyre, and Hiram Abif; and the five representing the classical orders of architecture – the Doric, Ionic, and Corinthian of Greece, and the Tuscan and Composite of

Rome. The last set represents the seven arts and sciences of grammar, rhetoric and logic – three attributes of language and communication; then arithmetic and geometry – two of the five classic sub-divisions of mathematics; then music and astronomy – an art based on the mathematical progression of harmonics, and an observational science based on the laws of physics and in particular those of gravity, but one which studies the almost infinite aspects of the creation of the Great Architect or Grand Geometrician.

In several US Masonic lodge rooms there are staircases in lodge rooms which are built with three flights of steps, first a series of three, then five, and then seven steps – fifteen in total. Each step has a symbol or name on it: the three have symbols of the square, level and plumb (also indicating the three stages of life – youth, manhood and old age); the five are named after the five senses - hearing, seeing, feeling, smelling, tasting; and the seven are named as in England. The winding staircase also has what is called the Bajan explanation, which gives a divine and human interpretation of the staircase. The first flight of three steps represents the divine wisdom, power and goodness, and also the human reason, will and emotion. The flight of five steps represents the five ancient forms of matter – earth, fire, water, air and ether, and also the five human senses by which they are perceived, as in the USA. The last set is of the standard seven liberal arts and sciences, but also referred to are the seven forms of life: lichen, vegetable, reptile, fish, bird, beast, and man. The great lesson to be learned, it is said, is to use all reason, will and emotion, all sense and matter, all art and science, as steps by which to ascend to the sanctuary of truth. It is always interesting to see the different interpretations of the symbolic meanings of the steps.

After this in some lodges the second degree charge is also delivered to the candidate. It is quite remarkable that this charge, after he has been given the freedom of investigating nature and science on a global basis, again concentrates on behaviour in lodge and with our fellow members. It is noted that the candidate has earned his promotion to the rank of Fellowcraft, which is an interesting comment if his passing has occurred at the lodge meeting immediately following his initiation. However, of the seven liberal arts and sciences, he was told to consider especially the science of geometry.

Thereafter the advice covered behaviour in lodge and with other members, and finally as another possible prelude to the next degree, '… on no account to wrong them or see them wronged …' – it is quite remarkable how inter-connected the degree ceremonies are. And as a reminder of this inter-linking, the candidate may have had rehearsed for him the questions and answers he needs to learn before going through his third degree. As before, this will have been performed by the members of the lodge, and will comprise the candidate's homework before the next ceremony.

The closing of the lodge from the second degree also includes some significant words from the Junior Warden, if closing in full – and why not always close down from the second degree in full for the new candidate, as it a short ritual? The words are 'Happy have we met; happy may we part; and happy meet again.' These words echo the quotation sometimes seen on the lodge summons, or on menu cards for Old English Nights, as it comes from the address to the brethren on nights of installation: '… to unite in the Grand Design of being happy and communicating happiness.' It is worth emphasising that we are here to enjoy ourselves, and to let some of that enjoyment rub off onto others; sometimes we can seem to take ourselves too seriously.

## Aftermath

At the festive board it is unlikely that the new Fellowcraft will have to respond to another toast to his health. He will again have been congratulated on taking his second regular step in Freemasonry by the Master, members and visitors, and he may this time have had the presence of mind to thank the Deacons in particular for escorting him around the lodge. He may also have thanked any member who delivered a particularly memorable piece of ritual, perhaps the explanation of the tracing board or the working tools if it were the longer version.

Having become more attuned to the workings of Freemasonry, he will doubtless again have several questions about what he has just gone through, especially if he has been advanced to this higher degree within one month or even after a few months of his initiation. He may query what exactly is meant by 'the hidden mysteries of nature and science'? And how is he expected to go about his researches?

The reply may include the concept that his first degree concentrated on his immediate surroundings – his family, his new Masonic family in the lodge, the requirement to always consider doing what he can for those in need, and his own conduct in addressing these matters. The second degree gives him permission to interact with, study and learn from a wider range of external bodies and organisations. There is an interesting comment given in the address to the Wardens at their investiture during the installation meeting: '… what you observe praiseworthy in others, you should carefully imitate; and what in them may appear defective, you should in yourselves amend.' We can all learn from others, but we must first analyse what exactly they are offering, and decide whether or not it is something that we want or need to take on board, or is something that may suit their character and requirements but does not suit our own. Therefore the Fellowcraft is expected to study, research and analyse almost everything that he interacts with in life: his family and friends, his work colleagues and firms he and they interact with, organisations in his local area or within the country where he lives and even those abroad. He is asked to become more spatially aware and not to passively note such items but to actively assess and assimilate all that can be learned from them by way of improving himself.

On the Masonic level, the broadening of his horizons will include the hierarchy of Masonry. He knows his own lodge, and may have visited others in the area, but the organisation of local lodges into Groups, and Groups into Provinces, and Provinces into Grand Lodge can be explained to him. There are some comments in the appendix which summarise some aspects of this and may be of assistance. The visitors who attended his initiation or passing ceremonies were already have provided evidence of the wider Masonic world: of his Province, if they were from local lodges or other Groups; of Grand Lodge, if some Grand Officers were visiting; and of the worldwide fraternity, if some were from abroad. He may also be loaned a copy of the Provincial year book (a useful purpose for out-of-date copies that may be retained by the lodge Secretary to this end), which will indicate how many lodges and side degrees there are within his own Province, as well as listing the Provincial bylaws which probably go into more detail than his lodge bylaws.

Similarly a Grand Lodge yearbook indicates how many lodges there are in England and Wales. It also has a very brief summary of the history of Grand Lodge at the back of the book, and this may be another aspect of Masonry from which he could gain satisfaction. It may be that your Masonic hall has a library of books that Masons can borrow and read through. Or perhaps a neighbouring lodge has such a library, or the Group to which the lodges belong. Or there is 'Freemasonry Today' or 'The Square', which are periodicals with several articles of general interest as well as updates from Masonic organisations ranging from Grand Lodge to the Masonic charities. And for the more voracious of readers, there are various books that can be bought via the internet or at local shops, from Masonic publishers including Ian Allan Publishing, etc. Additionally there are research organisations such as Quatuor Coronati and Manchester and other lodges and associations of Masonic research who publish regular proceedings of their meetings. There really should be no shortage of reading matter that the Fellowcraft can delve into if he wishes to follow the advice of the degree and extend his researches accordingly.

# The Member after Raising

## Introduction

The first two degrees have concerned themselves with the basic and practical aspects of being a mason, those workers involved in the physical building of structures. The third degree represents something different; and with the working tools being those used by an architect when he designs, scales and draws up a detailed plan, and also sets out the boundaries of the physical footprint of that structure on site, it represents attaining the upper echelons of the commercial building trade. Rather than concentrating on the practical day to day aspects of working on the site, it moves into that sphere of work where overall design and long term planning are required. This is in addition to translating those plans into detailed guidelines for those working on the actual construction of the building.

At the same time this degree ensures that the candidate moves into contemplative mode. Previously he has been encouraged to consider his immediate surroundings in the first degree, and then to widen his perspective in the second degree – always moving upwards in the size of the next Russian doll. Now he turns his attention inwards on himself and what he considers to be his core values, the innermost Russian doll. Until now he has been taught how to interact and behave outwardly, which to some extent can perhaps be effected in a mechanical way, while a person's behaviour should be a reflection of what he truly feels inwardly.

There is a quotation from Heraclitus, a Greek poet and philosopher of the Fifth century BC, in the Accessories' series of posters. Called 'The Light of Integrity', the picture on the poster is of the outskirts of a coniferous forest looking outwards at the sun shining in. The words are particularly apt: 'The soul is dyed the colour of its thoughts. Think only on those things that are in line with your principles and can bear the full light of day. The content of your character is your choice. Day by day, what you choose, what you think, and what you do is what you become. Your integrity is your destiny; it is the light that guides your way.'

Adopting a method-acting route of becoming a good citizen is a possible way of fitting into society and of being accepted. But to a large extent this limits the development of the unique person that is within the automaton, regardless of any external success. And internally we will always be driven by motive, and the teaching of Masonry is that as well as specifying acceptable and honourable conduct towards and with others, it includes the training of the mind and the development of the inner character.

The undoubted centrepiece of the third degree is the re-enactment of the death of Hiram. As has been said before, the message is not one of salvation by resurrection; that is the domain of religion. But by contemplating the fact that we have a limited lifetime in this existence, how do we want to plan the remainder of our lives? What do we want to have achieved before our life is over? And how do we want to be thought of once we have departed this mortal existence? Sometimes only by looking at the endgame can we decide how we want to live and operate before that time inevitably comes.

As an example, I used to run in the school cross-country teams. I was never outstanding at the sport on the national scale, but we had strong teams and I would be up among the leading finishers in inter-school events. And I was lucky enough to be in the winning cross-country relay team in the annual Midlands' schools event. In Coventry where I lived we had a nationally-recognised running club, Godiva Harriers, and Basil Heatley was among its leading members. Over the years the club had some world-class long-distance and marathon runners, and I always fancied competing in a marathon one day. But at university I found I was not good enough for the college cross-country team, let alone thinking of representing the university, so I concentrated on tennis and squash at a more social level, and the latter I played for some 20 years after leaving university. Then time moved on, and work became more time-consuming, and apart from some occasional walking in the Pennines and Lake District, sport took a back seat. And as I neared my sixtieth birthday I remembered that erstwhile goal of a marathon. If I didn't do something about that goal soon, I would probably be unable to ever compete in one. So I did a year's training, and took part and finished in the Salt Lake City marathon in 2008 – I have to admit by more walking than jogging, but I finished and raised some money for charities in the process.

Now we have major marathons around the world – London, Boston, Chicago, etc., and thousands of people taking part each year. Some of the participants want to show that they had recovered from major and life-saving operations, some are disabled, and each competitor has his own goal to achieve. The point is that you need to plan early on how you will achieve any goal, and that entails looking back from some point in the future and determining how you will get there and succeed in your endeavour. And also, as contained in the degree third, 'Be careful to perform your allotted task while it is yet day' – don't leave it till too late; procrastination is not an option.

Masonry, and especially the third degree, makes you assess yourself and your goals. It adds the condition that it not only achieving your goal, but the manner in which you have attained it. In other words, the end does not always justify the means. If your inner character and feelings are not attuned correctly to how you behave in public, then eventually there will be a breakdown between the two, and your true motives will be laid bare for all to see – the full light of day from Heraclitus.

## Recalling the Degree Ceremony
### Presentation

To the candidate, the degree started very similarly to the second degree. Another series of questions and answers, followed by an entrusting with another pass or passing grip and word, and then outside the door of the lodge to the tender mercies of the Tyler. The preparation there was very simple; just adding that of the first degree to that of the second in the way of adjusting the clothing, and the candidate was ready to re-enter the lodge.

And immediately something was different. Having passed through the second degree in full light, the blindfold of the first degree had been replaced by very dim lighting that had almost the same effect. There was perhaps a feeling of foreboding in the candidate that something a little more serious that the other two degrees was afoot.

The perambulations were probably to be expected, they crop up in every degree and their number usually equals that of the degree, and there was also the same freedom of expression as occurred in the second degree when interacting with the Wardens. The formal steps by which to progress to the east were increased again in number from those in the first and second degrees, and are also the most difficult of the three degrees to perform (virtually impossible when following the Emulation ritual to cover a forward distance of 6 feet), and this was followed by the warning that what was to follow was to be taken seriously.

### Obligation and Enactment

Then came the long obligation – the longest in the three degrees. It covered not only the priority of attending lodge, but also dwelt on the support and assistance to be given without question to any other Master Mason – basically emphasising the importance of team work and excluding no member of the team from these duties. The implements on the Holy Book had been adjusted again in order to reflect on the candidate's new status as a Master Mason in the Masonic hierarchy; perhaps this time he had noticed before it was pointed out to him.

Thereafter came a retrospect of the first two ceremonies. The first degree represented birth, man's duties to God, and his care for his fellow man. The second represented the intellectual aspects of life, and the wider experience by studying and interacting with all things in our world and even the universe, by which we can interpret and understand some aspects of the Grand Designs of the deity. And then came the contemplation of the individual on his inevitable demise, as seen through a re-enactment of an occurrence before King Solomon's temple had been fully built.

At the end of this enactment, which in some lodges is enhanced by a reading from the Old Testament, the candidate was brought back to reality and was asked to think about what he has just undergone, to step back from the brink as it were. The key word here is 'contemplation'. The candidate was told that this would direct his thoughts or reflections to a knowledge of himself. He was reminded that procrastination would achieve little, and would serve to almost ensure his underachievement, and he was reminded to continue to use all of his experience to interpret for himself the best way forward in any circumstances.

## Demonstration and Explanation

The first three signs of the degree were then communicated, and the penal sign was aimed at a part of the anatomy below those parts referred to in the second and first degree penal signs, which again seems to be a logical progression. The grip leads to a five-fold series of actions which was involved several parts of the body in sequence, and was quite complicated to perform. Perhaps this was the reason that the candidate was not called upon to perform the sequence again under the scrutiny of the Wardens, as had occurred in the previous two degrees. The candidate may have wondered why two words were given instead of only one. It arose from the time that the Antient and Modern Grand Lodges were discussing amalgamation, and they had developed similar-meaning but slightly different words, and they could not agree which one should be dropped – so they kept both.

Unusually in the three degrees the investiture of the Master Mason's apron was not performed until he had returned to the lodge. The standard comments of the Senior Warden are brief, but there is also a longer version that covers the two ribbons, the three rosettes, the five corners and the seven tassels and their symbolism – why introduce to someone a symbol and then not explain it to him fully? And the Master commented that although the new apron designates the candidate's new rank in Masonry, it also means that he is competent as a Master Mason and is also expected to give support and encouragement to the juniors of the lodge, be they Entered Apprentices or Fellowcrafts.

The re-enactment of the ceremony was then more fully explained in the traditional history, as seen through the eyes of those discovering both the crime and the perpetrators. In the USA this explanation is another enactment involving several more lodge members. Additionally the explanation of the derivation of the first two signs was woven into the story. The full five signs of the degree were then explained, and it is difficult to say if they were parts of one continuous sign, as each was discharged independently. Unlike in the first and second degrees, some of the international variants of the signs in the third degree were also presented, and the candidate did not immediately pass through the scrutiny of the Wardens, but moved on to the working tools of the degree.

These working tools are used, not by the general workmen, but by an architect or designer who is in charge of the overall build programme. The first tool was admittedly an implement to be used at the start of the build project, designating the overall limits of the foundations of the structure. The other two were both to be used on plans rather than on stones, and the symbolism of all three was explained.

And then in some lodges the charge in the third degree was delivered to the candidate. With so many pairs of nouns linked by 'and', the delivery is necessarily cumbersome, and this may be why many lodges have dispensed with it. The content was again mainly concerned with person to person interactions, with the heightened responsibility in the rank of a Master Mason of trying to 'improve the moral and correct the manners of men', in that you are to lead by example. Then in the second half of the charge the spotlight turned again upon self-awareness and the high principles inculcated by Masonry – the importance of remaining faithful to a person's central beliefs, and reflecting the message of the third degree ceremony.

Many Provinces have now introduced a short address that they wish to be conveyed to the new Master Mason, congratulating him on attaining the status of that rank of Mason, and also informing him about the completion of the degree will be given if and when he chooses to become a Royal Arch Mason. This may be delivered by the Master or a Past Master, or by a Group Officer who has attended the meeting specifically for this purpose.

So the third degree re-emphasises the lessons taught in the previous two degrees. In the first degree they encouraged you as a man to live honourably and discharge your duties to God, to country, to neighbour and to yourself. In the second degree they demanded square conduct, level steps and upright intentions as a code of conduct. Now in the third degree they point out that as a Mason you should retain your core principles even in the face of death, and that you should be prepared to support and defend every aspect of another Master Mason's honour.

Before leaving the ceremony, however, the formal closing of a lodge from the third degree called to mind the comment on the first two Master Mason signs in the traditional history. In their derivation and in the closing it was stated that they were substitute signs, and the Master says, as did Solomon before him, that they will suffice until the genuine ones are rediscovered. So although the candidate's voyage of discovery was apparently to be through the three Craft degrees, this implies that there is more to uncover. This acts as a prelude to Royal Arch Masonry, a side degree that follows on from the third degree, and as the mentor you can inform the candidate more about it, or let the Secretary give him some information concerning the possibility of joining after a period of time.

**Aftermath**

At the meal following the ceremony that new Master Mason was unlikely to have to respond to another toast to his health, but his new and personal apron will be a cause of congratulations again. And being a complicated ceremony, it is probable that he will take some time to digest the full content of what he has just gone through. Therefore as with other times in his development as a Mason, be flexible and go along at the pace that he is comfortable with; if you try to push him forward too hard, he may be forced to back away from active Masonry for a time.

After a short period of time, the lodge Secretary will receive from the Grand Secretary in London the Grand Lodge Certificate for the new member. He will be required to sign this in open lodge at the meeting when it is presented to him. If he is also given the explanation of the certificate, he will realise that it rearranges to some extent the explanation of the first degree tracing board which he may have heard before. If not, then it would be useful for his mentor to go through the design of the certificate with him, perhaps in the lodge room afterwards as another lesson in making him familiar with his surroundings when in lodge. He can also be advised that the certificate is best carried with his regalia, as there may be times when he is visiting other lodges that they are required to inspect his certificate before allowing him to enter the lodge. This is especially relevant if he intends to visit a lodge to which he has not been before, including those in London, and to do so unaccompanied by the mentor or other lodge member who might be able to vouch for him. It really is a passport to wider variety of visiting other Masonic lodges than he has previously been able to do. And remember the caveat, that the production of the certificate alone will not be sufficient proof that he is a Master Mason; the lodge will want to see the signs and tokens of the third if not all of the degrees, so the mentor should perhaps remind him how these are performed in his lodge.

There now begins the period before he starts on the ladder of lodge Officers – he may have a while on the sidelines before he becomes even a Steward – time perhaps to become bored, because he is not advancing in any perceptible way, and is obviously no longer in the spotlight as the subject of a degree ceremony. So it is essential that the mentor steps in to advise the Master Mason what he could be turning his attention to. This could be especially relevant if, as in many lodges, the new Master Mason was presented with a book of lodge ritual covering the first three degrees, and which he can now read through at his leisure, although he may need some assistance with the blanks.

This could be a time to consolidate what he has already learned about the Craft, and also to try to learn some of the longer passages of the ceremonies that will stand him in good stead when his responsibilities increase. Most people, having heard the different parts of their own ceremonies, delivered by lodge Officers and members from memory, have thought 'I could never do that.' And yet when they apply themselves, they can be surprised by how much they can retain and deliver in the lodge setting. Some people enjoy learning a story, and the explanation of the second degree tracing board and parts of the third degree are essentially this. Others will enjoy learning something that really struck a chord with them while they were listening to it the first time, and this could include the address in the north east corner or the charge in the first degree, or perhaps the long version of the working tools in the second degree, or the explanations of the three degree tracing boards – that of the third degree being embedded in the traditional history.

Not only will they be able to achieve a sense of satisfaction in mastering a part of the ritual, but they will also be flagging up to the senior members of the lodge that they are prepared to work at the Masonic ritual and become part of the team that performs the ceremonies. One of the early tasks frequently given to new Masons is to learn the working tools of each degree. In fact it is always a pleasant touch in any ceremony that a fairly young (Masonically) Mason can deliver part of the proceedings to the candidate – the message is that 'I was recently standing where you are as candidate tonight, so I have undergone almost all of the emotions that you are now feeling'. Some lodges always explain fully the working tools to the new Master at his installation, and often ask the junior brethren of the lodge to deliver these. And this may be his first formal step onto the lodge floor, to deliver rather than listen to a piece of ritual.

And it should be noted to the young Masons that, if they really want to understand any piece of Masonic ritual, they need to learn it and then deliver it to another Mason. If they don't understand what they are saying, then it is unlikely that anyone else will, and that piece of ritual could descend into a virtually meaningless piece of prose to be delivered parrot-fashion, rather than being an important part of the moral teaching of Masonry.

Many lodges have junior practices for the Masonic youngsters, and this is a time when people can try out parts of the ritual without the deadline of performing at an imminent ceremony. One may be asked to learn two paragraphs of the obligation of a degree, or take the Deacon's role and parade the candidate around. This not only allows the newcomers to learn some ritual, but also to obtain a feel for the degree ceremonies and their choreography which sitting on the sidelines can never achieve. There is little pressure on the participants, except that of wanting to perform well oneself, and it is a great place to try things without the book – nothing drives home what you have not learned properly than when you are standing there requiring prompts for what you thought you already knew.

If the lodge only has practices for the lodge Officers to go through their roles in the coming ceremonies, then there may be a lodge of instruction being held in the area by another lodge, and they will usually welcome outsiders who want to learn more about performing the ritual. In any case, the mentor, proposer or seconder, or lodge Secretary or Director of Ceremonies should know what other lodges in the vicinity have to offer, and they will be happy to give advice. If there is nothing in the area that fulfils this role, then they may agree to a one-to-one session, or even convene a meeting for a few interested people to meet together and go through parts of the ritual, and perhaps explain the meanings behind the different items. It is rare that they will pour cold water on someone who is willing and eager to learn and participate in lodge activities to a greater extent.

There is also one ceremony which the new Master Mason may not have encountered before, and that is the installation of a new Master of the lodge. It is in effect the annual birthday party of the lodge, and is often not far removed from the anniversary of the consecration of the lodge, and it normally attracts a bumper attendance of members and their guests. The dress code for this important meeting may be different from other lodge meetings, perhaps dinner jacket or morning dress, so warn your Master Mason. The new Master will be appointing and investing all of his new and continuing Officers, and it is a ceremony when all Master Masons, as well as Fellowcrafts and Entered Apprentices, are requested to retire from the lodge for the inner workings, which are restricted to Masters in office and Past Masters. This may be the time for several individual mentors to accompany the juniors outside the lodge, and there may be some useful discussions between those gathering there. If the individual mentors are themselves Master Masons, then they will be outside the lodge in any case. Many lodges lay on refreshments for those who have to wait outside, and sometimes those remaining within the lodge will join the others for a short refreshment break after the installation inner workings.

The installation is one of the occasions when several members of the lodge can play their parts in the different pieces of ritual that need to be performed. Often Past Masters are roped in to deliver the addresses to the various Officers of the lodge, although in some lodges the new Masters have to personally invest all of the Officers themselves. However, there are other pieces of ritual, such as explaining the working tools of all three degrees to the new Master. And what better way of confirming to him that he is going to be the head of a strong, supportive lodge, than for three juniors to deliver the three explanations to him. So perhaps the recommendation previously, to learn one or all of the working tools, will stand your Master Mason in good stead to be selected for this role, and confirm to the lodge members that he is keen to expand his horizons if allowed.

For some junior members there is the chance that the new Master will be their father or another family member. It would be particularly rewarding for him to receive one of the set pieces of the installation ceremony from his son or other relation, and the pieces of ritual can extend to the addresses to the Master or even to the brethren. There really can be no bigger stage on which the junior Mason can perform, and if he is confident about mastering the ritual, then give him the chance to shine – it may inspire him to even greater things in the future.

One of the first offices to be given relatively new members is that of Steward. There is normally a small band of such brothers who will serve at the meal following the meeting, and this may include leaving the lodge after the ceremony has been completed in order to make the final preparations for the meal, and setting out place cards and menus when appropriate. They will also wait on the tables serving drinks, and possibly serve the different courses of the meal and clear away the dishes afterwards. There may also be the selling of raffle tickets or other items to raise money for charity or other good causes, and these activities ensure that each Steward gets to know the members and regular visitors to the lodge.

If there is talent among the Stewards, then in some lodges they develop a team who can learn one or more of the old lectures that used to accompany the degrees in the early days of Freemasonry. Sometimes these are delivered in sections and sometimes as a question and answer session, and it will be something different from the usual ceremonies for the new Master Mason to apply himself to. There are minutes of lodges where such a team has been invited from another lodge to deliver the lectures, and this is a way of the Master Mason visiting other lodges and singing for his supper.

Apart from looking through the ritual, there are probably many activities in the lodge that the Master Mason can involve himself with. Unless there are a lot of Stewards, then they will always appreciate a helping hand with preparing the dining room, finalising the place settings, flowers, etc. The Tyler and Director of Ceremonies will always appreciate assistance with setting out the lodge room and tidying the furniture away afterwards.

The help with meals may also extend to lodge social events such as barbecues, where help with the cooking or serving of the food will be of use, and the social secretary may appreciate assistance with organising the function and transporting equipment and raffle prizes to the venue. It may be that, if the new Master Mason is keen on a sporting activity such as bowling (flat or crown green, or even 10-pin), the lodge could organise a bowling event which it has not done before, and here the Mason's contacts will be invaluable to setting the date and venue for such an event. As mentor you can ask your charge what activities he pursues in his own time, and then suggest to the lodge that it tries something different and that he can organise.

It may also be that the Master Mason brings a talent to the lodge from his work experience. If he works in the financial world, then he could become one of the lodge auditors or even the Treasurer, while if he has an IT awareness then he could help to set up or run the lodge website, and possibly assist the Secretary with setting up an e-mail database of members. If his talents run to graphic design and layout, then he could help with the design of promotional literature and flyers for lodge events, to be sent to members and other lodges, as well as the menus and place cards mentioned above. If the graphics expertise extends to table plans, then he could create the seating plan for the ladies' evenings or nights of installation, as these days there seem to be fewer people with the traditional calligraphy talents than in previous days.

The benefit of assisting in these ways is that the Master Mason not only feels that he is playing a constructive role in his lodge, but he is also interacting with members that he might not otherwise have done so. This will broaden his experience of people in the lodge and in Masonry, and they can in turn broaden his understanding of aspects of Masonry without him having to articulate the questions. In other words, he will be operating as a member of the lodge family, and will feel more integrated into it.

# The Member en route to the Master's Chair

The Master Mason has now been invited by the Master Elect to become an Officer in the lodge and on his team, perhaps as a Steward, or the Tyler or Inner Guard. And year on year he is promoted one step nearer to the Master's chair. So now there are particular parts of the ritual that he will have to learn – he can no longer pick and choose what interests him, although to most Masons all aspects of the ritual are interesting.

The lodge practices for the forthcoming ceremonies are now of more immediate concern to him, because he has to have learned his part fully so that the interactions between the lodge Officers, and the substitute candidate where appropriate, can occur seamlessly. It is preferable that no ritual books are visible when the final practice is being performed, and as has been said before, there is no better way of understanding what you have learned and what you have not learned than being stuck in the middle of a part of the ceremony at a loss for words. If this happens, it immediately highlights where further and immediate learning is required, and it is far better that this occurs in a practice meeting than in front of visitors and a candidate in open lodge.

So the Officer will have to concentrate on the lodge ritual, and this may be close to or very different from the Emulation or Nigerian rituals, which appear to be the default ritual books used by many lodges. If the lodge dates from the 18th century, then it may with pride have retained its own ritual based on the early days of the lodge. The mentor can ensure that the member obtains the correct ritual to learn from, whether directly or via notes of correction based on the nearest 'standard' ritual. There are many different rituals that can be obtained from Masonic publishers, and apart from the Emulation and Nigerian workings, there are others including Lancashire, Logic, Oxford, Stability, Sussex, Taylor's, Universal and West End. The Director of Ceremonies will know which ritual is followed in the lodge, and the Secretary may retain a few copies for new members.

And just as there are many ritual books covering all aspects of the Masonic ceremonies, there are also several books covering advice for each of the lodge Officers from Tyler to Worshipful Master. It is not proposed that in this book there will be a repetition of what can be read in those books – a selection of such books is given at the end of the book. However, some pointers as to what will be required may be of use at this juncture.

Learning the ritual is something for which each lodge member will have his own personal method, one which he has found by experience suits him best. Some will be able to memorise the ritual after a few readings, depending on the length of the text. Others will need to go through line by line and sentence by sentence and build up the full piece that they are required to deliver. And others still will prefer to have someone to listen to them as they deliver their ritual aloud, and would prefer not to be doing so in a full lodge practice. They might prefer one listener, who can prompt or correct in a quiet way – which would be an ideal role for his mentor. The venue might be at one or other homes of the two people involved, or even in the Masonic hall if there are rooms free on certain nights which can be used for such purposes.

Whatever method is tried by the new Officer, and he may try several before deciding what works best for him, the mentor assigned to him is the first choice of companion if time allows, and if not, then someone else known to the new Officer may be able to substitute. The key objective is to build up his confidence, in order that at the practice night he can give an assured performance, so be prepared to spend several sessions with him prior to the formal practice. It may be in time that a group of juniors band together in a team of learning and mutual support – which is just what was being taught in the third degree, so every credit to the people concerned if it happens.

Some lodges have foreseen this problem, and organise an informal lodge practice for the juniors, so that they do not have to be embarrassed by their first efforts, rather than just having the one lodge practice before the formal meeting. It may be that the Assistant Director of Ceremonies takes on the organisation of this meeting, but he would always appreciate some support, and may be grateful for a mentor that can stand in for him if he cannot make one of those informal practice meetings. Otherwise there may be one or two members, perhaps recently retired from full-time work, who can take on this aspect of mentoring, particularly if they have a reasonable mastery of the lodge ritual.

It also has to be said to the juniors who are learning the ritual, there is often no substitute for hard work and applying themselves to the task in hand. If they were to join a golf club for example, they would make sure that they were able to play on a fairly regular basis, otherwise the probably high subscription will be a waste of money. So if they can make time for golf, then it is far easier to do so for ritual. And there are many times that they will have a few minutes to themselves when another few sentences in the ritual can be assimilated. Perhaps they drive to and from work alone, and could use that time to improve their ritual. Perhaps they have a dog that requires regular exercise – there are reported to be several dogs in the country well versed in the three degrees, except for the delivery. Other people may enjoy country walks, even without a dog, and a short piece of ritual can be rehearsed during this activity. If they are alone at any time in the day, then that could be the time for them to pull out the little blue book and make some progress on what they have to learn.

When attending the lodge meeting as one of the Officers, it is essential that they understand the choreography of the ceremony to be undertaken and the rest of the lodge meeting. They may have spent a few years on the sidelines as an ordinary member or as a lodge Steward watching the ceremonies, and most of the time the different people have seemed to be able to interact seamlessly together to produce a near-perfect result. A warning should be stated here: it will all seem very different when the new Officer is on the floor, and nothing else is going to happen unless he performs his next part properly.

If the new Officer can understand the content of the ceremony, then it is often easier for him to be able to see how his role fits into the teamwork. The mentor can outline the choreography of the different parts of the ceremony as seen from the new Officer's eyes. The Inner Guard, for example, is always rooted at the door, so he has no movements to make except the signs in each degree. However, he does have to be alert to three sources of prompting for him to take action: the Tyler outside the lodge for warnings that someone, perhaps the candidate, wants to gain entrance into the lodge; the Junior Warden, to whom he reports and who asks him to see who wants to enter the lodge, and then he has to report the details of the incomers to the Master or the Junior Warden as appropriate; and thirdly it will be the Deacon bringing the candidate to be prepared or to redress himself, or coming to collect the candidate at the door.

The Inner Guard has to know if the incomers are properly dressed, so with the candidates especially he has to be aware of the correct mode of preparation. If he has served a year as Tyler, then he will know this from the times he has prepared candidates outside the lodge, but many lodges make the Inner Guard the first progressive office, rather than have a relatively new Mason stood outside the lodge when he could be soaking up the ritual inside. And comfortingly he is only the go-between for the Tyler and Junior Warden; he has no responsibility for allowing or refusing people entry into the lodge, as that pressure still rests on the Junior Warden.

The next office is Deacon, and here there is a certain amount of personal pressure. The Deacon escorts the candidate around the lodge, and prompts his replies to the various questions that will be put to him. There can be a word-perfect set of Officers and members taking part in the ceremony, but if the candidate is in the wrong place at the wrong time, then it all unravels quickly. So the Deacon needs to be aware that the number of perambulations in most lodges equals the number of the degree, and the last circuit is not commenced until the Master has instructed him to do so. The Deacon will need to know the dialogues with the Wardens in particular, as the candidate is always introduced by him, and he prompts the candidate's replies. He needs to be very careful with long words, if he expects the candidate to be able to repeat what he has said with confidence, so especially watch for a multi-syllable word to be given to the Senior Warden in the second half of the second degree.

The general routine for each of the ceremonies has been outlined previously, and is made up of the following:

**Presentation** – which includes the candidate answering any questions of the Master before retiring, admitting the prepared candidate, making the perambulations and interacting with both Wardens, and ensuring the candidate approaches the east in the required manner (the Deacon has to be able to demonstrate the correct method, according to the traditions of the lodge).

**Obligation and entrusting** – which includes prompting the appropriate answers after arriving at the Master's pedestal, ensuring the candidate repeats accurately what is being dictated to him in the obligation, placing the candidate in the correct position for being entrusted with the secrets of the degree, and ensuring he copies the actions and repeats or replies to the words that the Master states.

**Demonstration** – which includes escorting and introducing him to each of the Wardens in turn to be examined, and ensuring he performs the parts of the signs in the correct order and replies to the questions posed, and placing him ready to be invested with his new apron.

**Explanation** – this includes the symbolism of the apron, awaiting any comments from the Master after the investiture, placing the candidate at the appropriate parts of the lodge for further addresses or charges or the explanation of the working tools, escorting the candidate to and from the lodge door and ensuring he makes the correct signs (and they are often different when leaving and entering the lodge), and placing him ready for the explanation of the tracing board or other remaining items of the ceremony.

It all breaks down into a simple sequence of events, but one which most Deacons will have to practise several times before they are able to perform them confidently and without attracting some frantic hand signals around the lodge – often emanating from the Director of Ceremonies – that he should be somewhere else. The mentor can be the candidate in any one-to-one practices as well as on lodge practice nights, so that he can help to build up the confidence of the Deacon quietly and quickly.

In most lodges the two Deacons operate together for some parts of the ceremony, and then one or other has sole charge of the candidate for other parts. Thus the Junior Deacon is watching and combining with the Senior Deacon at several meetings, so the following year in the higher role is generally more enjoyable than that of the previous year, because it is his second year in a similar office.

The same training by experience comes with the two years spent as Junior and Senior Wardens. The duties encompass the beginning and the end of every meeting, in the opening and closing of the lodge, and each Warden has an alternate dialogue with the Master. The Wardens also have to follow the Master's knocks, in calling for silence or when signalling the opening or closing of each degree. They have to rise when addressed by the Master, with the appropriate salutes, and possibly need to propose the acceptance of the lodge minutes or accounts, etc. They additionally interact with candidates, in the presentation and the demonstration parts of the ceremonies, and they can do much to calm the nerves of both the candidate and the Deacon – with a quiet reassuring smile or the equivalent. The interactions are quite formal, but they do not have to be inquisitorial. In any case, the two years as Deacon ensures that those interactions are already understood, and will not take a great deal of additional learning when a Warden.

There may also be set pieces which are traditionally delivered by a Warden. In many lodges the charge after initiation is the responsibility of the Junior Warden, the working tools may be delivered by either, and the investiture of all aprons rests with the Senior Warden, who may also have the charges of the second and third degrees to deliver. So the quantity of ritual to be assimilated may represent a significant increase from the short sentences and perambulations of the Deacons. This may be the time when the mentor can go through the longer pieces of ritual with the Officer, and accordingly boost his self-confidence that he is able to undertake that responsibility in an assured manner.

It may be that your lodge has a formal lodge of instruction, or another local lodge has one that the Officer could attend. They will normally try to accommodate all brethren who want to improve their technique and delivery, although you need to check that they follow the same ritual as your lodge. Not many Directors of Ceremonics welcome one of the lodge Officers performing his role after the style of a ritual other than that of the lodge, so as mentor you need to be aware of such potential problems and advise the Officer how best to cope.

And finally the Master Mason attains the Chair of King Solomon as
**Master**. The highest accolade in the lodge is to be elected and
installed as its next leader. The whole basis of Freemasonry is laid
out to encourage each and every member, if at all possible, to work
his way up to the premier position in the lodge. There are more
books published with advice to the Master than to any other
Officer, and quite rightly, as he has to be aware of so many things
in and around his lodge. And with the top job there is a veritable
army of mentors lined up in front of him to help:

**Immediate Past Master** – ready with instant advice and counsel
   when required;

**Director of Ceremonies** – who will ensure that every meeting goes
   as well as possible, and that you have all the support from the
   team of Officers for the year;

**Secretary** – who ensures the smooth running of the lodge,
   regarding its returns, room bookings, meal bookings, and
   accommodation of dignitaries when visiting;

**Treasurer** – who can advise on all aspects of lodge finances and
   what the Master can afford to do in his year – and by the way, the
   Master is responsible for the well-being of the lodge; the Treasurer
   only looks after the money;

**Almoner** – advising the Master about the welfare of all members
   and their families as appropriate, especially those who would
   enjoy a visit from the head of the lodge in his year;

**Charity Steward** – who can organise all sorts of fund-raising events,
   to make the Master's year in office a landmark for the lodge.

And yet I have an idea that every Master will appreciate the quiet advice of a good friend who has shepherded him through all of the previous years – his mentor. Out of the glare of the limelight in a lodge meeting, most Masters would welcome a rest and relaxation session, where a calm assessment into how things went or did not go could be discussed on a one-to-one basis, and more importantly the creation of an action list if not a full action plan to ensure things go better next time around. It is a rapid learning experience being in the chair of a lodge, and in some ways it seems odd that just when each Master has 'mastered' the duties, he hands over to his successor.

So as a mentor, do not feel totally discarded. The Master's bandwagon swings into action each year, and many of the above-named people may take the burden of some duties away from the Master, so that he can focus on the essentials that he has to personally address. In my first lodge the demand was: 'In your year you will take the Master's role in the first, second and third degrees and in the installation; if we have another ceremony in any of the degrees, you may delegate.' And I assume that many other Masters have been met with that same welcome, even if it always was their intention to lead all three degree ceremonies at least once in their year.

Some can rise to the challenge and will enjoy doing so, others will need to be coaxed along and encouraged to take each meeting in small bite-sized chunks and assemble them all together on the night. And coaxing and encouraging are second nature to the mentor, so be on call for whenever you are required, and check periodically if you have not been approached for some time after the Master's installation. And the mentor has seen his protégé in almost every mood from elation to despair over the years, so he can tell from the warning signs that assistance is required, even when the rest of the Master's entourage don't necessarily recognise them.

Hopefully the Master has become more confident in his own abilities over the years, and has grown and developed Masonically with each office, so that now at the lodge pinnacle he is virtually the fully polished article. And if he can look you in the eye and say he <u>will</u> do the next task competently, then you will know that he has developed the inner resolve and capability to make things happen, and as a mentor you have done your job well. And whilst he has always been encouraged to develop at his own speed, keeping a balance between Masonry and the responsibilities of family and work, this may be the time for the individual mentor to back away and let him make his own way in the future. You will always be on hand for any advice, as will the lodge mentor, but just as the young birds eventually fly from the mother's nest, eventually each Mason will spread his Masonic wings and see how he fares on his own in the wider world.

# The Member after Occupying the Chair of the Lodge

After being Worshipful Master the lodge member moves to Immediate Past Master (IPM). He is still seated in the east, at the side of the Master and ready to assist in prompting the ritual and advising on the protocol of running the lodge meeting as required. So he is still keenly occupied in lodge activities, especially in the lodge ceremonial, and must be ready to stand in at short notice if the Master cannot attend a lodge meeting or practice or has to be at another event. On his collar he still wears as a jewel the upturned right-angle, but one with the addition of a square with right-angled triangle engraved onto it, and his collar now has a silk stripe down the middle to show his Past Master status.

But the following year there is suddenly a vacuum. After four years of being a Principal Officer and then IPM, there are no immediate demands on his time. Of course, some will enjoy a less demanding role for a while, in order to recharge their batteries, and will not mind becoming a back-bencher for a while. But it would be unusual for them to be satisfied with that lack of activity for very long. By the way, after his year as IPM, some lodges kick him outside the door of the lodge as Tyler, so he may not be immediately idle.

This really is a time for the lodge mentor to become involved, rather than the individual mentor. The lodge mentor will have an overview of all aspects of the lodge requirements and the capabilities of its members. He will know when one of the long-term Officers is wanting to step down, and probably will also have some ideas of who among the Past Masters might be capable and keen to take on the job. And it is always beneficial to try to fit a round peg into a round hole.

The individual mentors in the lodge will have been liaising with the lodge mentor as to how each of their charges is developing and what interests he has. Someone with a financial background might welcome a chance of becoming lodge Treasurer or Charity Steward. Someone with excellent people skills may want to tackle lodge Almoner, while someone with a good organising mind might want to be Secretary and gain a personal insight into how to interact with the Provincial office. And someone who has coped well with all of the ritual might jump at the chance of becoming Director of Ceremonies or his Assistant.

Additionally, and perhaps as the members were climbing the office ladder to the Master's chair, the Secretary and Director of Ceremonies – who both interact regularly with most if not all members, will have noted their capabilities and interests, and have passed on their own opinions as to future office holders. The lodge mentor is central to the collation of this information. This role may previously have been undertaken by the father of the lodge, but not every father has the time to do so; sometimes they hold senior Provincial or Grand rank, and are asked to represent at the meetings of other lodges, or perhaps they are a Group Officer and have to consider the welfare of several lodges. So a lodge mentor has a relevant role to play in this assessment exercise.

And if the Past Master is not going to take over a lodge office, what else can he do? If he were a good ritualist, then he might be directed into learning one of the major pieces of lodge ritual. These could include the charges at the end of each ceremony – with the first being the longest by far; the explanations of the first or second degree tracing boards, or the traditional history in the third which contains the equivalent; or the presentation of a Grand Lodge Certificate. These capabilities would come in very handy on a Past Masters' night, even though these types of meetings are more rarely seen these days, but he could also be a dependable substitute for the Director of Ceremonies to call on if someone else has to give backword (i.e. has to retract a previous agreed commitment) at short notice. And the older members might like to see the surprise on the faces of the eager lodge youngsters, when they hear a flawless delivery of a piece of ritual that they have thought about tackling themselves but have not yet attempted it. You may not be able to teach old dogs new tricks, but some of the old tricks are worth revisiting from time to time!

Among the Past Masters may be some people who have retired recently, whether early or at sixty or sixty-five. They may be looking for additional challenges. Some of them these days will have useful computer skills, so why not point them in the direction of creating a newsletter for lodge members, or a website for members to obtain the latest update on lodge activities, whether as firm dates in the calendar, or events with an eye towards forward planning.

If one has an interest in history and documents, then it could be that the lodge history requires updating. It is always useful if each generation keeps the history up to date while it is happening, rather than leave it to someone ninety-five years after the lodge was founded to try to piece things together. So armed with any lodge histories that already exist, he could try to continue the record, and might suggest additional information that could be included in a future edition. He may also read about some aspects of the past and the previous members, and decide to investigate further how they operated within the Province and what Provincial duties they undertook. This information might serve to paint a fuller picture of some of the characters from the early days of the lodge, who undoubtedly helped to mould the lodge into its current form.

One or two Past Masters may enjoy interacting with the youngsters in the lodge, and may jump at the opportunity of becoming an individual mentor to a newcomer. We are attracting new members of all ages, and a more mature entrant may appreciate a more mature mentor being assigned to him, and leave the youngsters to interact together. They will certainly have the experience which will be useful to pass on to the new Mason, and you as lodge mentor will have formed a view as to whether or not they are good communicators and have a circle of friends into which they do not mind introducing a new member, which may make accompanying him when visiting other lodges a more enjoyable event for him and them.

If they have retired and have interests such as gardening or fell walking or similar activities, then they might look into organising a visit by members to a major garden show, or a trip to the Lake District to climb some of the peaks there. Every member will bring a set of unique talents to the lodge and, if pushed gently and wisely, the lodge could gain a wider enjoyment of life by bringing those talents into use. We are all part of a Masonic family, and the organising of such events may extend beyond the lodge and also involve other lodges and members of the Group, where there will undoubtedly be other people with similar interests who will combine to enjoy the activity together. And if the Past Master has not yet been to the headquarters in Great Queen Street in London, then he would perhaps enjoy organising a trip to the museum there, possibly timing it to coincide with a meeting of Grand Lodge or arranging a visit to one of the London lodges meeting there, or at Mark Master Masons' Hall or at one of the other venues in the capital.

And if the Past Masters have a wide circle of friends within and around the lodge, and enjoy meeting and chatting with their contemporaries, then let them assist the Almoner in ministering to those in need. Often the greatest boon to people recovering from illness or an operation is to have someone to visit them from time to time and talk about all sorts of things, Masonic or otherwise. In fact they may make up a car club and take turns to drive a group of people to see lodge members who are not as mobile as they were. And some members will not be able to drive any more, and the offer of a lift on these occasions or to lodge meetings would enable them to continue to enjoy their Masonic interactions as they did in their younger days.

In all probability the need for a mentor is now past, and the once new Mason all those years ago can now stand on his own feet. He has discovered a great deal about Masonry, and has developed his own personal interpretation of it and knows what he enjoys and wants to do. He will always appreciate a chat with the person who looked after him in his early days, and will occasionally bounce ideas off you for guidance, but you have helped him to find his feet in Masonry and done the job well. And when did you suggest to him that he might become a mentor to someone else, and pass on his enjoyment of the Craft to a new member? You didn't? Maybe you should remember it for the next time around.

# Handing over the Duties of Lodge Mentor

The duties of the individual mentors or coaches will end when the Mason being helped is able to stand on his own feet. This will be by mutual agreement, although as stated before, in many cases a lasting friendship will have been formed.

Having said in several places that as lodge mentor you may well be acting with the individual mentors or coaches for different newcomers into the lodge, there will probably be one at least who has shown a natural aptitude for this work. Care must be taken that he has the time, along with his family and work commitments, to broaden his responsibilities to more than one newcomer, because it would be a shame to overload someone who has a real talent by increasing his workload too quickly and thereby causing premature burn-out.

The lodge mentor has a role in some aspects equivalent to several other lodge Officers, in that he interacts closely with other members of the lodge. In this sense so do the Director of Ceremonies, the Secretary, the Charity Steward and the Almoner, for example. Each has to know the other lodge members well enough to be able to interact with them, persuade them to assist in ceremonies or in the organisation of the lodge, fund-raising, and visiting brethren who are not able to come to lodge.

The individual mentor will have an enjoyment in what he does – interacting with people, helping them to gain more from Masonry, perhaps accompanying the juniors on visits to other lodges, etc. But you would not want your successor to be an identical clone of yourself, and neither would the lodge. A change of officer should be like a breath of fresh air, capable of bringing new life into the job. This does not mean that there should be change for change's sake. The capable successor will doubtless retain whatever has worked well for you and him in the past, but will shade aspects of the whole job according to his own interpretation of the task involved.

So why not let such a person perhaps be taken under your wing as the lodge mentor, and perhaps sit in some meetings – with the Secretary and Director of Ceremonies for example, and listen to the discussions about the progress and talents of the different members. As an individual mentor he might have been involved with this type of activity before, and he should be able to understand the benefits, for the person and the lodge, of such meetings to plan for a succession in the various offices that need to be filled within the lodge.

And when there are any meetings with the Group or Provincial Mentor, then take him along with you and let him see for himself how mentoring is co-ordinated in the Province. He has to feel confident about taking on the higher role, but you cannot keep him in this state of being an understudy for too long. Quite soon you need to step aside and let him fly on his own. Both you and he will know that you are only a telephone call or e-mail away from being contacted for any advice required, but the arena should be his within a reasonably short time of becoming your understudy. And if for example you are stepping up to Group or Provincial Mentor, then there will be regular and continued interactions with him in any case.

If all goes well, you will congratulate yourself on selecting the right man to replace you in your lodge position, and both that man and the lodge will be very grateful for all of the work – mainly unobserved by the majority of members – that you have contributed to the success of the lodge and its members over the years, and for having made provision for its successful continuation for many years to come.

Of course, if you have particularly enjoyed the job as lodge mentor, you may be asked to become the Group or even the Provincial mentor, and you will have to leave your immediate lodge responsibilities behind. You will now have to bring your experience to a number of different lodges, and maybe visiting several you have not been to before. You will also have to organise the training and information meetings for the lodge or Group mentors, and possibly be interacting with mentors from other Provinces. There is always something to be learned by listening to what has succeeded elsewhere, and it can be a useful way of refining and sometimes redefining the way you have been operating in the past.

Retiring from these more elevated positions will be similar to retiring from the lodge mentorship. You will probably have noticed some very capable Masons who could take over your job, although you will only be able to advise who might succeed you. However, with all of your experience, it is unlikely that you will not be consulted about your potential successor, as he will probably be drawn from the people with whom you have been interacting for a while. And there is a rewarding feeling that you are leaving a position that has contributed to the continued and perhaps improved good health of Masonry in your area, for which I hope you will receive due acknowledgement.

# Appendix

## The Workings of a Lodge

To some extent this is for the initiate beginning to learn about the Masonic world, and on the night of becoming an Entered Apprentice, his lodge is the total extent of his Masonic world. Some aspects of the Officers' roles and duties and the lodge surroundings and operation are given below in summary detail, while in other places there is reference to information already gathered into a readable format elsewhere. It is not expected that all of this explanation is necessarily given to the new member in one session, and in any case there may be documents containing similar summaries of other aspects that the initiate can read for himself, perhaps with a little additional explanation from the mentor.

## Lodge Officers

Starting at the top of the list of Officers on the summons there are:

## Master

He sits in the east behind his pedestal and obviously controls the whole proceedings within the lodge, announces the successive items of business, and calls on other Officers to deliver their reports. He also opens and orders the closing of the lodge, and often personally conducts the ceremonies for candidates. The most important job within the ceremonies is the obligation, but he often conducts other aspects such as the questions before a degree, the north east corner, etc., although in more recent times there has been an increase in this work being shared among other members of the lodge. He will also preside over the meal afterwards and, with his lady, over any socials that the lodge holds; while in other activities he will act as chairman of the lodge committee and any other meeting of lodge members in his year, including the interviewing of candidates. He is addressed as Worshipful Master, in the same way as the Mayor of a town is addressed Worshipful, and after his year of office he retains the title of a Worshipful Brother. All brethren not having occupied the chair of their lodges are called simply a Brother, and when addressing a lodge Officer it is Brother Secretary, etc. Everyone in the lodge room, when addressing the Master, will salute him with the sign of the degree the lodge is operating in, and some lodges call upon the Master to repeat the sign as an acknowledgement. His jewel is an upturned square hung from the apex, although in some older lodges it is a 'gallows' or square hanging from the shorter arm.

## Senior Warden

He is, as his title implies, the second in importance of the three Principal Officers, and sits in the west behind his pedestal. He follows the Master in sounding his gavel to call for order in the lodge, and he is requested by the Master to formally close the lodge at the end of a meeting. He has a column of office on his pedestal (often surmounted by a globe of the constellations of stars in the heavens), which he places upright to show the lodge is formally open, and lowers it to the horizontal when the lodge is closed or called off. He is one of the interrogators of candidates during ceremonies, both on their first or more perambulations before being obligated and also to test the new knowledge of the candidates afterwards. It is he whom the Master requests to dress the candidate in his higher rank apron after proving that he has taken in the lessons of the degree through which he has just been elevated. He also answers the Master's knocks at the meal after the meeting and at socials if there are any speeches, etc., and if the Master is indisposed for a length of time, it is the Senior Wardens who will call for the issue of the summons for the next lodge meeting. His jewel is a level.

## Junior Warden

He is next in importance to the Senior Warden, and his is the third knock heard in a lodge and elsewhere when calling for order and silence. On his pedestal in the south he has a column of office (often surmounted by a globe of the earth), which he places horizontal to show the lodge is formally open, and raises it to an upright position when the lodge is closed or called off. At the installation you will hear included in the address given to him that he is the 'ostensible steward' of the lodge, and at one time it was the Junior Warden who looked after the lodge finances and paid for the meal and drinks after the meeting from the lodge cash box. Nowadays he and the Treasurer together ensure that the lodge Stewards are performing their duties conscientiously at the festive board. He is also charged with checking that every attendee at the meeting is a properly documented Mason, and this will include testing any latecomer to the meeting, for which he may retire from the lodge to personally check the credentials of the stranger if no-one in the lodge room can vouch for him. He is normally the lodge member who will propose the toast to the visitors at the meal afterwards. His jewel is the plumb rule.

## Chaplain

His job is to deliver the prayers at any lodge meeting, both the openings and closings in the first and second degrees, and in all of the three degree ceremonies, and in the installation. He also has the job of saying grace before and after the meal. Interestingly it is not his job to open and close the Bible in the lodge meeting, that duty being left to the Immediate Past Master. Perhaps this is a reflection of the traditions of some of the early lodges, when the Master would be required to say the prayers if the Chaplain were not present to do so. Masonry has always laid great store in the belief in a Supreme Being, the lodges being considered to stand on holy ground, and all obligations being taken in a kneeling position. Thus the Chaplain is the first appointment after the Wardens, and his jewel is the open Volume of the Sacred Law.

**Treasurer**

It is to him that the new member's joining fee and subscription was paid at the initiation. He oversees the accounts of the lodge and collects the annual subscriptions from all members, from which he pays the Grand Lodge and Provincial Grand Lodge dues, as well as any fees for using the Masonic hall for meetings and other gatherings. He is an elected Officer rather than being appointed by the Master on the night of installation, and he has to keep records of all monetary transactions into and out of the lodge account. He also has to prepare the annual accounts, and submit them to the lodge for approval (BoC153), normally within six months of the end of the lodge financial year. In doing so he will work with and be scrutinised by two other lodge members who, although not being formal Officers in the lodge hierarchy, are appointed annually as auditors. His jewel is a key, perhaps being an emblem from the lodge cash box that would have been used in the early days of Masonry.

**Secretary**

It was he who invited the new member to his formal interview with lodge members, and who submitted the lodge declaration book for signature on his night of initiation. He brings to the attention of the lodge all reports and correspondence from Grand Lodge and Provincial Grand Lodge as well as items of general business, and it is he who issues to each member the summons for each lodge meeting that is convened (BoC145). He also records and publishes the minutes of all transactions at one lodge meeting to be approved by the members present at the subsequent lodge meeting (BoC144), and may also record the business of the lodge committee meetings. He ensures that the several returns to Grand Lodge and Provincial Grand Lodge are sent on time (BoC146). He keeps up to date all of the appropriate personal contact details of each member, such as address, telephone number, e-mail address, etc., and that a membership list is issued as required to the lodge members so that all can keep in touch with one another. If any member cannot attend the next lodge meeting, it is a courtesy to inform the Secretary, who will formally note your apologies and pass on the warning of your absence to appropriate people like the Director of Ceremonies, and will also ensure that the meals after the meeting are not over-booked. His jewel is two crossed feather quills, harking back to old days of ink and parchment records of lodge business.

## Director of Ceremonies

It is he who sometimes seems to run the lodge meetings. Indeed he has charge over the choreography of the meetings, ceremonies and festive boards, and who tries to ensure that all participants are conversant with what is required of them and when. He is often seated close to the Master, who may want to refer to him before moving on to the next business of the meeting. He will normally have a sound knowledge of the lodge ritual and traditions, and is required to introduce and where appropriate salute all important dignitaries who visit the lodge (and those in the lodge). He may have interacted with the candidate at times during the ceremonies, or he may have left all escorting duties with regard to the candidate in the hands of the Deacons, while in some lodges he may personally escort other members who participated in those ceremonies to where in the lodge room they delivered their observations or charges. In fact he is the third person of the trinity – with the treasurer and secretary – by and through whom the lodge is organised, and it is probably not coincidental that these three are ranked together in senior positions in the lodge hierarchy. He often carries a wand or in some lodges a baton, and his jewel is a pair of crossed wands, as seen on his collar and on the top of his wand.

## Almoner

He is the lodge member charged with looking after the welfare of all of the members of the lodge. It is often stated in the lodge summons that the Almoner should be notified if any member, or his partner or family, is ill or has any similar problems. He will liaise with the member concerned, and try to ensure that whatever support the lodge and Masonry can provide is there when required. He can ensure that a member who is ill is visited by members of the lodge, and if monetary assistance is required for operations or convalescence, then various Masonic funds can be approached to provide relief. This can extend to providing funding towards the cost of operations, or for medical appliances required to live as full a life as possible after operations, continued welfare in retirement, as well as helping in times of bereavement and the aftermath that the family has to endure. Also included there may be assistance for the widows and children left behind by a late member, and also help with the continued schooling of the member's children, boys and girls, which may include going through university. This was a responsibility formerly charged to the Master of the lodge, but which duty of care was transferred in the early 20th century to an individual who would be able to look after lodge members for a period greater than a yearly basis, and thereby provide the continuity of care required. The member selected for this office has to have great care and tact, to be able to deal with a wide range of very personal and confidential situations that can arise. His jewel is a scrip purse with a heart on it.

**Charity Steward**
He is the member who encourages the lodge members to raise money for charity. Charitable giving was highlighted in the earliest days of Masonry, and was another duty placed on the Master, who often organised what was called the Master's list of charities, which would be supported by the lodge in his year of office. Again in the 20th century another lodge member was given this task, after the groupings of lodges were made to co-ordinate the fundraising for

the new headquarters at Great Queen Street in London after the First World War. As the festival system of raising money for national Masonic charities was introduced afterwards, the Charity Steward became the focus of lodge activities to that end and the link between the lodge and Group and Provincial hierarchy. The fundraising can extend from major charities to local organisations, and these are often discussed and it is agreed by the whole lodge as to where their efforts should be concentrated over the next months and years. While acting as a charitable conscience in the lodge, it must be added that such giving should always be within the means of an individual, having catered for himself and his family first, and so will vary from member to member according to their individual means. Wherever possible, he should encourage the use of Gift Aid donations, whereby the tax previously paid by the individual can be recovered by the registered charity, which boosts the amount given by over 25% while not costing the individual any more. His office also requires some tact, in balancing an enthusiasm for raising funds from members, but not overdoing it. His jewel is a trowel, the traditional symbol in Masonry for spreading the cement of brotherly love and relief over and within the whole organisation.

## Senior Deacon

He has charge of the candidates for most of the ceremony of passing (the Junior Deacon may look after the candidate at the start of the ceremony), and throughout the ceremony of raising (in the USA he has charge of the candidate in all of the three ceremonies). He will also accompany the Junior Deacon around the lodge during the initiation ceremony, and will often work with him in adjusting items of lodge furniture at the opening and closing of the different degrees. He sits near the Master, and at the opening of the lodge his duty is stated as conveying all commands from the Master to the Senior Warden and there to await the return of the Junior Deacon. In many lodges he will carry the minute book from the Secretary for signature by the Master and the Senior Warden, but will let the Junior Deacon do the same for the Junior Warden. He may also convey other items as required from the Secretary/Treasurer's table, and this could include the alms dish or bag for the charity collection, and the ballot box for any ballot to be taken within the lodge. He carries a wand around the lodge room, and his modern jewel is the dove bearing an olive branch, which is seen on his collar and at the top of his wand. In some of the older lodges his jewel is a figure of Mercury, the winged messenger of the gods.

## Junior Deacon

He is the lodge Officer who conducted the candidate on his initiation night, who instructed him on where to walk and how to commence walking, and who dictated almost all of the answers that the candidate had to give during that first ceremony. He also assists the Senior Deacon in the passing and raising ceremonies, and the two may operate together during the opening and closing of the different degrees (in the USA he has no escort duties, but is effectively the Inner Guard of the lodge). He is seated next to the Senior Warden, and at the opening of the lodge it is noted that he conveys all communications of the Master from the Senior Warden to the Junior Warden. In many lodges this will include the carrying of the minute book for signature by the Junior Warden, and he may also assist the Charity Steward and the Senior Deacon in the collection of alms in the meeting. He also carries a wand around the lodge room, and his jewel is the same as that of the Senior Deacon.

## Organist

His job is self-explanatory. Most lodges will sing an ode or hymn at the initial opening and final closing of the meeting. Some lodges have additional pieces of music, perhaps relating to different times in the various ceremonies, and may also play music while the minutes are being carried around the lodge and other pauses in the meeting. Organists are generally in short supply, and if your lodge has one he may be in popular demand and will often be invited as a guest organist in other lodges. His jewel is a lyre, which was a kind of harp and dates back to Roman times.

## Assistant Director of Ceremonies

He is essentially the understudy of the Director of Ceremonies, and he may undertake parts of those duties in lodge. When doing so, he will also carry a wand with him. The jewel on his collar and on his wand is the same as his boss, except that the word 'Assistant' is superimposed on the crossed wands.

## Assistant Secretary

He is also an understudy, this time obviously of the Secretary. Again he may have some delegated duties, such as reading the minutes of previous lodge meetings, and perhaps recording the minutes of the lodge committee meetings. His jewel is the same as that of the Secretary, except with the word 'Assistant' superimposed on the crossed quills.

## Inner Guard

It is he who allows people to enter and leave the lodge room. Indeed it was his voice that the initiate first heard from inside the closed lodge room, when trying to gain admission. He is told in his installation address that he should check people's attire before they enter the lodge room. When the lodge is opening or closing in a degree, he answers to the Junior Warden, whose duty it is to assess whether or not any visitor is qualified to enter a lodge when opened and in session. The Inner Guard may also participate in the processions at the start and end of the meeting, and at these times he often accompanies the Tyler in the perambulations. His jewel is a pair of crossed swords, and he will have a poignard or a short sword in his hand for ceremonial purposes – some of the older lodges armed the Inner Guard with a trowel, as they refused to have any weaponry inside the lodge room.

## Stewards

They are the lodge members who often spring into action at mealtimes. In some lodges they will leave the lodge before the end of the meeting, in order to lay out the festive board and serve all of the courses of the meal, as well as waiting on the tables to ferry drinks from the bar to the lodge members and their guests. If there are waiting staff in the Masonic Hall, then the lodge Stewards may content themselves with serving the wine and other drinks. At the installation they are reminded to see that all members and visitors are properly accommodated, and in so doing they will effectively work with the Junior Warden as ostensible steward of the lodge, and if additional beverages are required, then also with the Treasurer. Some lodges also call upon their Stewards to substitute for any of the junior Officers who are absent from the lodge meeting, and this may be an occasion when the young Steward can take an active part in a degree ceremony; if they have studied the different roles, then they are more likely to be asked. Their jewel is a cornucopia or horn of plenty, and the smooth running of the after-meeting proceedings is essentially down to them.

Some lodges choose to designate the person at the top of the list of Stewards as the Chief or Senior Steward, although this is not a formally recognised position. Those lodges who wish to recognise his seniority often delegate specific duties to him: perhaps leading the Stewards of the evening out of the lodge room to prepare for the meal, or perhaps taking the meal bookings, organising the table plans and collecting the dining fees prior to the meeting. Other lodges may delegate the formal laying out of tracing boards and other furniture in the lodge to him, either in conjunction with the Tyler and Director of Ceremonies or performing the tasks alone. In American lodges it is the two principal Stewards who prepare the candidate for the coming ceremony, though in England this is left to the Tyler and/or Deacons.

## Tyler

He is the first Mason to interact formally with the candidate on the night of his initiation ceremony. He therefore has a unique opportunity to form a friendship with any newcomer to the lodge in that year, or any candidate going to a higher degree. His duty is to guard the entrance to the lodge, and check that all visitors and attendees are bona fide members of the Craft, and that candidates are properly prepared for the three degrees and sometimes also for the installation ceremonies. His role in the lodge has always been of great importance, and traditionally he is one of two Officers elected by the members of the lodge rather than being appointed by the Master, though this may have originated when several lodges elected a non-member of the lodge as Tyler, so that all members could be in the lodge room to discuss any matters of importance together. In such circumstances his services would be paid for, and hence his election to that post was a joint decision of all members rather than being left to the head of the lodge. These days there are still lodges that vote for a non-member to hold the office, perhaps in a Masonic hall where the same gentleman may perform the Tyler's duties for several lodges. In many lodges, when the tyler is a member of the lodge, he is appointed by the Master at the installation. His jewel is a single sword.

The offices of Tyler (sometimes), Inner Guard, Junior then Senior Deacon, Junior then Senior Warden are commonly known as the progressive offices of the lodge, in that most lodges expect their members to have filled those positions prior to their election to be the Master of the lodge.

## Immediate Past Master

He usually sits at the left hand side of the Master, and was in almost all cases the Master in the previous year, as the name implies. He is not a lodge Officer, as he gained his title from his deeds in the previous year. He is close to Master in order to prompt or advise him if required (often the Director of Ceremonies is close by for the same reason), and if the Master is unable to attend the meeting, then the IPM will normally occupy the Master's chair in the east. Sometimes there are formal duties that the IPM will perform, perhaps opening and closing the Bible on the pedestal and adjusting the square and compasses as required, and he is sometimes tasked with delivering the traditional history in the third degree. Indeed, the lodge is not regularly opened until the Volume of the Sacred Law is opened, and it is closed whenever the lodge is called off or closed for the attendees to go to refreshment. His jewel is the upturned square, within which is hanging a representation of the 47th problem of Euclid, represented by a right-angled triangle.

There are several books written that cover the many aspects of the various lodge offices and spell out the duties and how to discharge them in much greater detail. These are a useful source of reference if more detailed discussions may arise, or the new member wants to read around the subject more. A selection of these is given at the back of this book, and additional information is available though the Provincial office or from the bookshop in Great Queen Street.

## Warrant of the Lodge

Displayed somewhere in the lodge room will normally be the warrant of the lodge. Interestingly this does not belong to the lodge, but to the Grand Master (BoC102), and must be returned to him if the lodge ceases to meet. The warrant must always be in the lodge room or at least on the premises, and in the cases of the older lodges which might already have centennial or bicentennial warrants these cannot be used as a substitute – they are only warrants of confirmation. In the early days the warrant was given to the Master of the lodge during his tenure, and it was his responsibility to bring it to every meeting – some lodge minutes have recorded that the lodge meeting could not be held because the Master forgot the warrant (BoC101). Nowadays they are frequently framed and left in the lodge room or in an anteroom and brought out on meeting nights, but at the installation of a new Master he is still told that the warrant is being delivered into his special keeping, and should be kept safe in order to hand it on to his successor. It should also be noted that, although traditionally the number of Masons making a 'perfect' lodge is seven, the Book of Constitutions now requires nine regular Officers, while the warrant has to be handed in to the Grand Master if the annual return shows less than five members (BoC188).

**Lodge Summons and Literature**

The new member will have seen the lodge summons, at least on the night of initiation, and there is a wealth of information included therein. Apart from the list of the current Officers, there are often listed the previous Masters of the lodge, sometimes going back to the earliest days of the lodge. In some Masonic halls these names may be listed on boards in the corridors or in the lodge or dining rooms, and there may have been local dignitaries including Mayors of the area, senior businessmen, famous sportsmen, local squires, etc., numbered among them. The new member will receive a copy of the summons prior to each subsequent lodge meeting (BoC145).

There may be a logo of the lodge on the front of the summons. Often this is a replica or is based on the lodge banner, which may hang permanently in the lodge room, or may be stored separately and only brought out for meetings, especially in a shared lodge room. There will undoubtedly be some symbolism in what is depicted on the banner, and perhaps there will also be an explanation of the message that its designer or creator was trying to convey when it was being made.

While in the lodge room, there will be many items of furniture whose purpose is not immediately obvious. A guided tour around the room may be helpful for the new member to be able to establish his bearings in his new Masonic home. Some items may have been gifts from previous members of the lodge, or indeed other lodges if the room is shared, and several may have interesting stories to be told about background reasons for the gift. Some lodges have a diagram of their lodge room and where their Officers are seated, but if you are able to walk around the lodge room with the newcomer, so much the better. It may be worth inviting him to attend early at the next lodge meeting, so that you can quickly go over the layout again as a reminder.

In one lodge room where I am a member there are light brown wooden cubes instead of white balls to go with a set of black balls. These arose from a time when one of the mother lodge's members was going blind, and to vote in a lodge ballot using two sets of balls may have been awkward – the cubes gave that member with hardly any sight the opportunity of voting correctly as he wished, and so that he was able to participate fully in lodge affairs. This is a minor example, but one representing the brotherly consideration for others that the early lodge members deemed to be appropriate, and still do.

If you want to explain the various items around the lodge room, you should turn to the back of the ritual book on Emulation working, where there is an explanation of the first degree tracing board. This is really a walk around the lodge room, and explains the symbolism of many of the items contained therein. Although the new member will normally receive this ritual book or another one after the third degree, there is no problem with the mentor reading though it beforehand or noting extracts from it while going around the lodge with the new member. Another item that the new member can look forward to is receiving his Grand Lodge certificate after his third degree, and the engraving depicted thereon is very similar to what is incorporated into the first degree tracing board. As there will be ready access to a printed copy of both explanations, no further comment is necessary in this book.

There may already be existing booklets or books about the history of the lodge, which the new member can borrow to browse through at his leisure, even if there are no additional copies that the member can keep for himself. These will give him an insight into why the lodge came into existence, who were the founders and perhaps from what walks of life, and some of the highlights of the years though which the lodge has ploughed its furrow. The lodge may also have mothered several offspring, and it may be able to trace its existence to its own mother lodge and beyond. This may also be an early introduction to the wider Masonic family of which the new member has now become a part. These lodges may meet in the same building or further afield, in which case a future visit to one or more of them could be planned.

**Toasts at the Festive Board**

At the meal after the lodge meeting, sometimes called the social or festive board, there is a traditional series of toasts as follows, which may include (the meal after the installation meeting may include toasts not honoured after the other lodge meetings):

The Monarch and the Craft.

The Most Worshipful Grand Master (currently the Duke of Kent).

The Most Worshipful Pro Grand Master;
The Right Worshipful Deputy Grand Master;
The Right Worshipful Assistant Grand Master;
and the rest of the Grand Officers, Present (acting rank) or Past.

The Right Worshipful Provincial Grand Master.

The Deputy Provincial Grand Master;
The Assistant Grand Masters (if any);
and the rest of the Provincial Officers, Present and Past.

The Master.

The Installing Master.

The Founders, Past Masters and Officers of the Lodge.

The Newly Initiated Brother.

The Masonic Charities.

The Visiting Brethren.

The Tyler's Toast.

# The Workings of Provincial Grand Lodge

The new Mason may have already noticed and commented on the darker blue aprons worn by several members in the lodge, rather than the light blue of Master Masons and many lodge Officers and some Past Masters, and he has been told that they are worn by Provincial or Grand Officers. More rarely are seen the red-edged aprons of Provincial or Grand Stewards. Provincial rank is conferred on Masons as recognition for their services to Masonry in their locality. Mainly the honours come to Past Masters after a certain amount of time since occupying the Master's chair of their lodge; perhaps six to nine years is common, but sometimes they are awarded to non-Past Masters for similar services. It is expected that those services will continue after the honours have been bestowed, rather than the Mason will rest on his laurels, and if they continue to work for Masonry then later there may be promotions in Provincial rank.

England and Wales have forty-seven Provinces, each headed by a Provincial Grand Master and his Deputy. The first Provincial Grand Master was Col. Francis Columbine, appointed over the Province of Cheshire in 1725. In the main the Officers of the year have equivalent titles to the lodge Officers and perform similar duties, except the lodge Inner Guard becomes the Provincial Pursuivant. There are some additional offices, the major one being that of Assistant Provincial Grand Master. This is a fairly recent office, being created in 1920. In the larger Provinces, there is one Assistant Provincial Grand Master appointed for every 40 lodges (BoC67). At the time of writing this book, the largest traditional Provinces include West Lancashire with 407 lodges, Essex with 333, Surrey with 319, and East Lancashire with 291. These Provinces therefore have 10, 8, 7 and 7 Assistant Provincial Grand Masters respectively.

The smallest Provinces are Jersey with 11 lodges and Guernsey & Alderney also with 11, then Herefordshire with 14, and the Isle of Man with 17, but each has the full Provincial team of Officers excepting any Assistant Provincial Grand Masters. The larger Provinces are also able to appoint more than one of some acting Officers, for example several Senior and Junior Deacons, and Assistant Directors of Ceremonies.

The Provincial Grand Master is appointed by the Grand Master with the power to act in every way as Grand Master in his Province, and with very little reference to London in doing so (BoC63). One of the main responsibilities of the incumbent is in the consecration and continued well-being of the lodges under his jurisdiction, and more recently to oversee the amalgamation or the complete demise of some of his lodges. The investiture of a new Provincial Grand Master will normally be conducted by a senior Officer of Grand Lodge but rarely by the Grand Master himself, and such an event is a major celebration in the Province, with many heads of the neighbouring Provinces in attendance. The standard period of office used to be five years, but it was also renewable for further five-year periods. Nowadays the period of tenure of the position is not enumerated in the patent of appointment. Some Provincial Grand Masters have continued for many years; for example RWBro John Hale retired from that post in Cumberland & Westmorland Province in 2008 after a term of 22 years.

The Provincial Grand Master appoints his Provincial team for the year at the annual Provincial Grand Lodge meeting (BoC78) and invests them, and all of the appointments are for the year only. Even the Deputy Provincial Grand Master has to be reappointed in the following year, along with the other longer-term Officers such as the Provincial Secretary, Treasurer and Director of Ceremonies. To be appointed into acting Provincial rank is one of the greatest honours that can be conferred on a brother. In the larger Provinces, with a large number of official visits to be made during the year, there will be several Deacons, Assistant Directors of Ceremonies, Stewards, etc., appointed, but there will always be a leading Officer who will take that post at the Provincial meetings. The number of additional Officers who can be so appointed is laid down in the Book of Constitutions (BoC68).

In the smaller Provinces the Provincial Grand Master may well be able to visit all of his lodges regularly if he chooses. In the larger Provinces, once there are 260 lodges, he could spend every weekday visiting his lodges once each in a year, but he doesn't have the time. There are other Provincial duties and meetings, and attending the Grand Lodge quarterly meetings and the annual meetings of neighbouring Provinces, which make this impossible, and this is why he is empowered to appoint the Assistant Provincial Grand Masters to help him and his Deputy to visit a large proportion of his lodges each year. When there are several Assistants, they will often be allocated to look after certain areas of the Province, but where there are only one or two they will probably help on a Province-wide basis.

It should be noted that the largest Provincial Grand Lodge nowadays, with about 1500 lodges, is the Metropolitan Grand Lodge which covers London and the immediately surrounding area. The London lodges used to be governed directly by the Grand Master and under the supervision of the Grand Secretary until 2003, when on 1 October RWBro Lord Peter Millett was appointed as the first Metropolitan Provincial Grand Master. He has recently been succeeded by RWBro Russell Race. The Metropolitan Grand Lodge also has a Deputy Metropolitan Grand Master, but has fewer Assistant Metropolitan Grand Masters than one for every 40 lodges, having only three assigned to the Craft. Below them are the Metropolitan Grand Inspectors with about 100 lodges each, then below them there are the Senior Visiting Officers, and below them there are the Visiting Officers with the number of lodges that they have oversight for being in single figures.

The Provincial Grand Master also has the power to confer Past Provincial ranks onto members of his Province. The most frequent recipients are Past Masters of their lodges, some years after leaving the chair, and their rank will reflect how important their contribution has been to Masonry, and has continued since leaving the chair. These appointments are also conferred at the annual Provincial meeting, and there is normally a large attendance of lodge members to see one or more of their brethren receive their honours, but there is the restriction that attendees have to be Master Masons. The number of past honours that can be given each year is generally in proportion to the number of lodges and Masons in the Province, and because in the larger Provinces both totals are falling, the number of such honours each year is also decreasing. Metropolitan Grand Lodge operates in a different way, appointing Masons to only one of three levels: London Grand Rank some years after going through the chair of a lodge, promotion to Senior London Grand Rank some years after that, and London Rank for those people with meritorious service but who have not been the Master of a lodge.

One of the happiest duties of a Provincial Grand Master is to supervise the consecration of a new lodge. The full Provincial team turns out for this special ceremony and, with the Founders of the lodge and their many guests, it makes a colourful spectacle. In current times the number of consecrations throughout the country has diminished to a low number, which is hoped will be somewhere near the bottom of a long-term cycle, but if there is a consecration in your area you should try to attend and witness it for yourself. There is a restriction that you have to be a Master Mason to do so, as the ceremony is conducted under the authority of the Provincial Grand Lodge.

Next down in the Provincial organisation, where necessary, are Groups or Districts, which may cover perhaps 15 to 50 lodges, and these cover separate geographic areas within the Province. Each

Group has a Group Chairman appointed by the Provincial Grand Master, and in the larger Provinces it will usually also have a designated Assistant Provincial Grand Master under whose jurisdiction it resides, with perhaps two or three Groups clustered together in this way. It was in 1914 that the Groups were first created in the Province of West Lancashire for example, with the Province being divided into 22 such Groups, and there are a similar number still today.

And next down in the structure come the individual lodges. This means that there is a structured organisation between every lodge and its Provincial Grand Master. This hierarchy is very useful when it comes to cascading information down from the Provincial office, or routing problems or requests for clarification upwards. The system also confers the ability to sort out local affairs locally, rather than having to bring in the full Provincial machinery on every occasion.

One of the benefits of such a system is when raising money for the Provincial charities. All Provinces have at least one Provincial charity fund, and some have several for different purposes, perhaps one to assist aged Masons and another to assist in the provision of health care, etc. From time to time there will be a fund-raising appeal on a Province-wide basis for one of these charities, and the Group Chairmen and Assistant Provincial Grand Masters will be encouraging as many events to be held in their region when the proceeds will go towards the appeal.

Additionally about every 11 years the Province will organise a festival in aid of one of the major four national Masonic charities: the Grand Charity, the Royal Masonic Benevolent Institution, the Royal Masonic Trust for Girls and Boys, and the Masonic Samaritan Fund. The fund-raising will take place over a number of years, and then there is a festival banquet when the monies are handed over to the recipient charity. During this time each member of the Province can pay additional funds that will entitle him to wear a festival jewel, and this will also entitle him to be present at the banquet festivities.

With regard to the organisation of the Province, it will issue a year-book, normally during the summer so it is ready for the start of the winter season. This lists all of the lodges, chapters and other side degrees in the Province, and some contact details should anyone want to visit another lodge or a meeting of an order beyond the Craft. It also lists the recent Provincial appointments and promotions, and notes all of the Provincial charity organisations. Additionally the bylaws of the Province are written out in full, and will usually be much more detailed that the lodge by-laws (the new Mason has read the latter, as requested at his initiation, hasn't he?) The Provincial bylaws give a useful insight into how things are organised in the Province, and also the time by when the various lodge returns have to be submitted.

Some Provinces also organise training and/or educational events. If there is a lodge of Masonic research or association in the Province, then they may organise some of them. Others will be for lodge Officers, for example workshops for the Directors of Ceremonies (yes, immaculate as they are in their deportment and mastery of the ritual, even they can sometimes benefit from some formal training!). If the subject matter is of interest to the newcomer that you are supervising, then contact the organisers and check if you and he can attend. For the general educational meetings there should be no problem, but for some of the workshops there may be limited accommodation, though normally the organisers will welcome someone keen enough to try to find out more about the different aspects of Freemasonry.

# The Workings of Grand Lodge

The ruling body in Masonry in England and Wales is the United Grand Lodge of England (UGLE). There are similar but singular Grand Lodges in Scotland and Ireland, and also in most foreign countries. The UGLE headquarters is in Great Queen Street in Holborn, London, and from there over 8,000 lodges and over 250,000 Freemasons are administered.

The Grand Master since 27 June 1967 has been HRH the Duke of Kent, and his investiture at Olympia attracted an audience in excess of 7,500 Masons from all over the world. Many of the Grand Officers have the same titles as their lodge and Provincial equivalents, and there is a Deputy and an Assistant Grand Master. However, because the Duke of Kent is a member of the royal family, he can appoint someone who is called the Pro Grand Master, and who will substitute for the Grand Master when he has to be away on royal or other business. Currently the Pro Grand Master is MWBro Peter Lowndes.

The day-to-day running of Grand Lodge falls to the Grand Secretary, who has three sections working for him: communications, finance and administration, and secretarial services. Above the Grand Secretary is the General Council, and its duties are summarised in the Book of Constitutions (BoC216-222) Within the Council is a body called the Board of General Purposes, which looks at longer-term issues, and covers finance, external relations (such as with other Grand Lodges), public relations, and disciplinary matters (BoC223-238).

Within the organisational structure there is also the Provincial Grand Masters' Forum, where matters are discussed relating to all aspects of the government and running of the Provinces, and it can refer matters to the Board of General Purposes and vice versa. It was this body that requested a working group to review what was happening with mentoring around the country, and as noted earlier, the group reported in a Grand Lodge meeting in 2008, and the work is ongoing.

There are nineteen Grand Stewards invested each year from the 'red apron' lodges in London (BoC36), which are numbered below:

No. 1, The Grand Master's Lodge (dating from 1756);
No. 2, Lodge of Antiquity (Time Immemorial, 1691);
No. 4 (IV), Royal Somerset House and Inverness Lodge
(Time Immemorial, pre-1717);
No. 5, St George's and Corner Stone Lodge (1730);
No. 6, Lodge of Friendship (1721);
No. 8, British Lodge (1722);
No. 14, Tuscan Lodge (1722);
No. 21, Lodge of Emulation (1723);
No. 23, Globe Lodge (1723);
No. 26, Castle Lodge of Harmony (1725);
No. 28, Old King's Arms Lodge (1725);
No. 29, St Alban's Lodge (1728);
No. 46, Old Union Lodge (1735);
No. 58, Lodge of Felicity (1737);
No. 60, Lodge of Peace and Harmony (1738);
No. 91, Lodge of Regularity (1755);
No. 99, Shakespear Lodge (1757);
No. 197, Jerusalem Lodge (1771);
No. 259, Prince of Wales's Lodge (1787).

The Provincial and Metropolitan Grand Stewards probably have their red aprons based on this Grand Lodge tradition. At one time the Grand Stewards had to organise the meals for the quarterly meetings of Grand Lodge, and make good any deficit of income over expenditure. As they did not have much control over the ticket price for attendees, they were not necessarily sought-after positions in the early days. Today the Grand Stewards still make up any shortfall arising from the Grand Festival dinner which follows the Annual Investiture of Grand Officers in April. The Grand Stewards' Lodge is placed at the head of the list of lodges, but it has no number (BoC99). Lodge No. 1 is the Grand Master's Lodge; Lodge of Antiquity No. 2, Royal Somerset House and Inverness Lodge No. 4 (IV) and Lodge of Fortitude and Old Cumberland No. 12 are the oldest lodges in UGLE and designated as 'Time Immemorial Lodges'; while the Lodge of Friendship No. 6 and British Lodge No. 8 are the oldest surviving lodges to be warranted by the Premier Grand Lodge, in 1721 and 1722 respectively.

The Book of Constitutions, possibly unopened since their initiation ceremony by most Masons, has a wealth of detail on the operations of Grand Lodge (BoC2-59), the hierarchy of its Officers, and its relations with Provinces in the country and Districts and lodges overseas (BoC62-91), and also with individual lodges under its jurisdiction (BoC94-191). The detailed communications expected each year from the lodges are laid out, as are the duties and responsibilities of lodge Officers such as the Master. Towards the back of the book the disciplinary procedures, hopefully infrequently required, are also set out (BoC272-280). Also included are the ancient charges that used to be rehearsed in some of the oldest lodges, and one or two of them are sometimes read aloud at the opening of several lodges for the benefit of the brethren. These cover much of the ground included in the charge after initiation but are presented in a different manner, so they are worth a look in their own right.

Grand Lodge also issues a year-book, which enumerates every lodge in England and Wales (as well as some in countries overseas) and their year of founding. At the end of the book there is also a concise account of the history of the Grand Lodges in England and Wales and the key dates therein. In brief, the First Grand Lodge was established in London in 1717 (followed incidentally by Ireland in 1725, and Scotland in 1736). Several rival Grand Lodges sprang up in England over the years, the major one being the Antients' Grand Lodge in 1751 (whereby the original Grand Lodge was accorded the name 'Moderns'). Then after several years of discussions, the Antients and the Moderns amalgamated on 27 December 1813 to become the United Grand Lodge of England (UGLE), hence the unusual name. There are many books covering the history of Freemasonry in England, but it is better to obtain the full detail from them rather than to have a potted history summarised in this book.

When the Premier Grand Lodge was inaugurated on 24 June 1717, it was decided that there would be held a quarterly communication or meeting, and Grand Lodge still meets on a quarterly basis, on the second Wednesdays in March, June, September and December. These meetings can be attended by those who are or have been Wardens and Masters of lodges and, if in active office, the Warden or Master should be wearing his lodge collar. There is an additional meeting in April when those who are receiving Grand rank for the first time or receiving promotion are invested. The year-book details all current holders of Grand rank and the years in which they were appointed and promoted, and it is a very select list. Masons having held very senior Provincial offices will receive them, and other Masons who have contributed to Masonry in a very significant way - if your lodge has a Grand Officer, then it is probably in a minority. Even if your lodge does not have a Grand Officer, it is likely that one will represent the Provincial Grand Master at the lodge installation meeting, so Grand Officers continue to work not just in their own lodge.

Also in the year-book are listed the Hall Stone lodges. After the First World War an appeal went out to English Masons to fund a new Masonic hall at Great Queen Street, called the Masonic Million Memorial Fund, the memorial being to the fallen in the war. Each lodge was told that if it could contribute 10 guineas (£10.50) for each member, then it would be given a Hall Stone Jewel, which was to be worn by the Master during his year of office. At the time the average weekly wage was only £2, so the contribution was over a month's salary before tax – perhaps nowadays being equivalent to about £2,000 or more, was no mean achievement, especially immediately after the war to end all wars. The foundation stone was laid in 1927 and the hall was dedicated six years later in 1933. The grand staircase and many of the meeting rooms have appeared in period films and television plays, and hiring out the facilities at Great Queen Street has been a useful aid to covering the running costs of the building.

The English Grand Lodge also has jurisdiction over lodges in several other countries. Many of these date back from when the British Empire stretched around the globe, and military lodges in particular were warranted to meet abroad in Europe, India, Africa, etc. When the military presence departed, often some of the locals who had joined kept the lodge going, still under English jurisdiction. In some countries there were only a few such lodges, and they continued to pay their dues to UGLE. Most foreign countries now have their own Grand Lodges, which historically subsumed most if not all of the existing lodges which had been warranted by the Grand Lodges in England, Ireland and Scotland. When the USA gained independence from Britain, the Grand Lodge in each state took over the running of the lodges with previous allegiance to the United Kingdom. Thus the oldest lodge in the Grand Lodge of Massachusetts, now No.1, was originally St John's Lodge No. 126 in Boston under the English constitution in 1733; Lodge No. 1 in the Grand Lodge of Georgia was originally Solomon's Lodge in Savannah numbered 139 in 1735; and this process was repeated in several other eastern US states. Similarly military lodges left behind in Europe transferred to the new national Grand Lodges when they formed. For example, Lodge No. 50

meeting at the French Arms in Madrid and warranted in 1728, is now the Matriteuse Lodge No. 1 in the Grand National Orient of Spain.

Care has to be taken when visiting lodges in overseas constitutions. UGLE does not recognise every Masonic Grand Lodge in the world, let alone quasi-Masonic organisations which call themselves Grand Lodges. Some do not insist in a belief in a Supreme Being, which is key to the English constitution. Others admit women as well as men, or consist of only women, and UGLE insist on men only. Even with these restrictions, there are around six million Masons worldwide, operating in many countries in the world. In the USA, for example, every state and Washington DC has its own Grand Lodge, as does every province in Canada and every state in Australia, except South Australia and Northern Territory are combined. All of these Grand Lodges are recognised by UGLE, but anybody travelling abroad and wishing to visit a lodge there should first contact his Provincial office to ask for advice, and they will address the matter or refer it to Grand Lodge. Without that check he could find himself in a strange organisation and be giving away our Masonic secrets by doing so – which everyone is obligated not to do during his initiation ceremony. Some lodges include a reminder in their summons to contact the Secretary or Province before arranging any visits to lodges abroad.

# The Major Masonic Charities

In English Freemasonry there are four major national charities, all based in London. These are: the Freemasons' Grand Charity, the Royal Masonic Benevolent Institution, the Royal Masonic Trust for Girls and Boys and the Masonic Samaritan Fund. As there will be charity festivals occurring more often than not within his Province in aid of one or other of these charities, the new Mason should be introduced to the concepts behind each of them.

## The Freemasons' Grand Charity
**60 Great Queen Street, London WC2B 5AZ**
**0207 395 9261; www.grandcharity.org**
*Helping with Financial Need*

The central charity of English Freemasonry started in its current form on 1 January 1981 as a successor to the Board of Benevolence, which itself had evolved from a series of committees formed for the relief of distressed Freemasons (the earliest being established in 1725). Each Freemason makes an annual contribution to this fund as part of his Grand Lodge subscription (over one-third of it), and those who are members of several Craft lodges make an additional contribution to the charity with each subsequent subscription.

Approximately two-thirds of its annual disbursements are given to individual Masonic petitioners, and sometimes grants are made to other Masonic charities as required. More recently the Grand Charity has taken over the financing of annuities to brethren and their dependents from the Royal Masonic Benevolent Fund. After taking over this responsibility, in 2002 for example it paid over £1.6M in 1194 grants – to help with daily living, utility bills, repairs to property and disability equipment, etc., and in the same year over

£4M was paid in housing grants. In 2008 the financial grants to Masons and their dependents had risen to £3.4M to improve the quality of life for 1,911 people. A more recent additional assistance is the provision of mobility equipment for those with limited walking capability, so they can keep a measure of independence, and these vehicles are loaned to the beneficiaries for as long as they need them.

The Grand Charity also makes major donations to non-Masonic charities, which was one of the reasons for changing its remit in 1981. The donations have included those to temporary disaster funds set up for the relief of victims of famine, floods, earthquakes, etc., and the Grand Charity is often one of the first organisations to be contacted by people setting up such relief funds, as its response is rapid and assists in ensuring the fund has some early working capital with which to commence the aid operation. Recent examples of the appeals supported have included the 9/11 tragedy in New York in 2001, the tsunami disaster in the Far East in 2004 (a dedicated relief chest has now donated nearly £1M in aid work), the Hurricane Katrina devastation of New Orleans in 2005, and the Haitian earthquake disaster in 2010. The disaster agencies are grateful for such immediate donations that help the very start of the relief operations, before the national and international governments can organise their full scale assistance.

Each year there are grants of £50,000 and more given to a variety of major national charities. Some have been regular beneficiaries, such as the Royal National Lifeboat Institute, which in over 134 years has had a total of twelve lifeboats donated outright as well as the lifeboat stations at Clacton and Hope Cove, and has also received smaller individual grants in the intervening years. In 1986 the Medical Hospital Foundation was given £250k, as was the Great Ormond Street children's hospital in 1987. At the start of the 1990s the Samaritans were given £500k over a three-year period, while in 1992 to celebrate the 275th anniversary of the founding of the first Grand Lodge, a total of £2.05M was donated to four national charities assisting people with learning difficulties: CARE (£1,250k), Home Farm Trust (£500k), Camphill Village Trust (£250k), and the Elizabeth Fitzroy Home (£50k). In the following year the MacMillan Cancer Relief Appeal received £500k. To celebrate the Millennium another series of charities were assisted at the end of 1999, including Crocus (now Beating Bowel Cancer) with £500k, Sargeant Cancer Care £446k, Crisis £405k, and Help the Aged £400k. In 2003 £100k was donated to the Institute of Cancer Research as part of a ten-year £1M total grant, while in 2007 over £235k was donated as immediate aid to various emergency disaster relief funds around the world.

Some of the grants to be given in 2009 were announced at the annual general meeting in June and totalled over £1.95M. They covered support for medical research, with grants of £250k to Moorfields Eye Hospital over three years, and £50k each to Diabetes UK and the Motor Neurone Disease Association. In the £210k given to organisations providing youth opportunities there was £60k to the Depaul Trust, £50k to Brathay Hall and £45k to Barnado's. To support those catering for vulnerable people £565k was provided, including £150k to Lifelites, £55k to Emmaus UK, and £50k each to Alzheimer's Society, British Red Cross and the Calvert Trust Lake District. And in the other grants there was £500k given to adult and children's hospice services and £192k to Air Ambulances.

**Royal Masonic Benevolent Institution**
**60 Great Queen Street, London WC2B 5AZ**
**0207 596 2400; www.rmbi.org.uk**
*Helping Older People*

The RMBI has been caring for older Freemasons and their dependants for over 160 years. Grand Lodge inaugurated the Royal Masonic Benevolent Annuity Fund for men in 1842 and the Female

Annuity Fund in 1849. The following year, 1850, the first Home was opened in East Croydon, named the "Asylum for Worthy, Aged and Decayed Freemasons", and the Royal Masonic Benevolent Institution (RMBI) was established. The Home remained in Croydon for over 100 years until 1955, when, due to the need for bigger premises, the Home was transferred to Harewood Court in Hove, East Sussex.

The financing of the RMBI, before the Provincial festival system of fundraising, had been by the generosity of individual Masons and lodges, as well as the Grand Charity as required. At the centenary celebration of the Institution in the Connaught Rooms on 25 February 1942, under the chairmanship of the Grand Master, the Duke of Kent, a sum of £96,500 was raised – a remarkable amount in the middle of the Second World War.

In the early 1960s, provision was extended to non-annuitants and, between 1960 and 1985, a further fourteen Homes were set up or acquired around England and Wales. These included the new residential Home at Oadby in Leicestershire opened in 1966 by Queen Elizabeth the Queen Mother, and in 1967 another at Cramlington, Northumberland, opened by Princess Alexandra. Thereafter followed new Homes in 1968 at Chislehurst in Kent, and in the 1970s at Fulford in York, Sindlesham in Berkshire, Porthcawl in Glamorgan and at Llandudno in Conwy. Five more Homes have been opened since then and two have closed, with the result that currently the RMBI operates seventeen residential care homes across England and Wales offering high quality care. Many of its Homes are registered for both residential and nursing care and a number offer specialist dementia care.

Limited sheltered accommodation is offered for those people who prefer to live more independently, but with support nearby in an emergency. The RMBI has a team of Care Advice Visitors, who know a great deal about health and welfare rights and benefits. They can also give advice on all aspects of the services offered by the

RMBI and the other Masonic charities, and by statutory and voluntary agencies. The RMBI can also offer short-stay breaks, including respite care. These are helpful for both those living alone, and for families that need a little respite from the demands of caring for an older relative. Some of the Homes have limited guest accommodation, which even so can be of great assistance to family members wishing to visit their relations and who themselves live a considerable distance away.

The RMBI believes in treating everyone as an individual. Every potential resident is assessed to find out what type of care package would best meet his or her needs. A tailor-made care plan is put together, which is reviewed on a regular basis. Residents who choose an RMBI Home have the security of knowing that they have a home for life regardless of any change in their financial circumstances, as long as their particular care needs can be catered for.

Additionally there are homes owned by Masonic Care Ltd, the Masonic Housing Trust and its sister organisation, the Compass Housing Association Ltd. These are separate from the RMBI but their homes offer similar facilities and are available for renting.

**Royal Masonic Trust for Girls and Boys**
**60 Great Queen Street, London WC2B 5AZ**
**0207 405 2644; www.rmtgb.org**
*Helping Young People*

The first charity for the children of Freemasons was set up in 1788, by the creation of a boarding school for the education of girls whose parents had suffered misfortune and who could not continue their anticipated education unaided. The education provision was free, unless the family's income was such that a contribution could be levied. The first school was built between Euston and St Pancras railway stations, and then moved to Westminster Bridge Road in

1795. A new building for the girls' school at Wandsworth Common, London was opened in 1852 by the Grand Master, the Earl of Zetland. Queen Victoria became the Chief Patroness of the school in 1882, and on 12 March 1891 the Centenary Hall and a new wing of the school was opened by the Grand Master, HRH the Prince of Wales and his wife, later to become King Edward VII and Queen Alexandra.

On 16 July 1930 the foundation stone was laid of the new Senior School of the Royal Masonic Institution for Girls at Rickmansworth in Hertfordshire, to the north west of London, and was formally opened by Queen Mary on 27 June 1934. The *modus operandi* of the school was changed in 1982 to become the Rickmansworth Royal Masonic School for Girls, offering education in the private sector and open to all girls while retaining some places for the daughters of Freemasons. The school is set in 320 acres of Hertfordshire countryside; the senior school currently accommodates 300 boarders and more than 400 day girls, and there are also 200 places in the junior school that cater for girls of 5 years and over.

The equivalent charity for the education of sons of Freemasons was founded in 1798, but the creation of a separate school for boys only occurred 65 years later when the foundation stone of the new schoolhouse at Wood Green, London, was laid by Algernon Perkins, PGW in 1863. In 1898 the celebration of the centenary of the boys' institution raised the sum of £141,000, and on 12 May 1900 the foundation stone of a new school at Bushey in north London was laid by the Duke of Connaught & Strathearn, who was installed as Grand Master on 17 July in the following year. On 8 June 1926 the foundation stone of the new Junior School at Bushey was laid by the same Grand Master. The school was finally sold in 1977, and the boys' charity fund reverted to providing for the continuing education of boys closer to where they lived rather than being based solely in London.

In 1982 the Trust Deed creating the Masonic Trust for Girls and Boys was signed and on 1 January 1986 the two Institutions were merged under this new title. In the following year an Act of Parliament ensured that donations made in favour of the former Institutions could be legally transferred to the new Trust. Permission for the additional title of "Royal" was granted in 2003. The mission statement is "To relieve poverty and advance the education of children of a Masonic family and, when funds permit, support other children in need." To qualify for support from the main funds a family must have suffered distress (for example from the death, disability or desertion of a parent) that has resulted in financial hardship. There must always be a Masonic connection; usually the qualifying Freemason is the father or grandfather, but in some cases it could be someone else who is a Freemason who can demonstrate that they are bringing up the child or children as their own.

Currently at the start of the 21st century the Trust is looking after about 1,700 girls and boys. Some girls are placed at the Rickmansworth School, for which there are entrance examinations, and others are supported at various schools around the country, as are all of the boys receiving assistance. The help can cover maintenance grants, fees, grants for books, clothing, food, accommodation, equipment and educational travel, and can extend to higher or university education and professional training. Information on the range of assistance and grants and scholarships from separate funds managed by the Trust are available by contacting its Secretary.

To celebrate the new millennium, the Trust launched Lifelites, a project for helping children's hospices throughout England and Wales. The project aims to improve the lives of young people with life-limiting illnesses by providing a full package of education and entertainment technology. The equipment given by Lifelites enables terminally-ill children who visit a children's hospice to continue their education, pursue their interests and activities and keep in close touch with family and friends.

In 2006 Lifelites was established as a subsidiary charity (Registered Charity No 1115655). The Trust appoints Trustees to Lifelites and provides administrative support. Lifelites continues to seek practical and financial support both from the Craft and from non-Masonic sources. Lifelites can sometimes arrange visits to the hospices they support if Masons want to see the benefits of their efforts firsthand. The Lifelites' offices are at 26 Great Queen Street, London WC2B 5BL; telephone 0207 440 4200; www.lifelites.org.

**Masonic Samaritan Fund**
**60 Great Queen Street, London WC2B 5AZ**
**0207 404 1550; www.msfund.org.uk**
**Email: mail@msfund.org.uk**
*Caring for the Health of Freemasons and their Dependants*

In 1843 a Masonic Fund was started in memory of the first Grand Master of United Grand Lodge, the Duke of Sussex, after his death on 21 April of that year, and was devoted to the Royal Free Hospital in Gray's Inn Road, London. The foundation stone of the new Sussex Wing of the hospital was laid on 30 July 1855 at an especial Grand Lodge meeting, and formally opened by the Grand Master, the Earl of Zetland, on 18 June 1856. During the First World War the Freemasons' War Hospital in the Fulham Road opened in the August of 1916, and later became the Freemasons' Hospital and Nursing Home, and a second War Hospital was opened at Fulham Palace in May 1918.

On 19 May 1932 the dedication stone of the new Freemasons' Hospital at Ravenscourt Park in London was laid remotely by electrical connection to Olympia, by the Grand Master, the Duke of Connaught & Strathearn, attended by 11,000 brethren. The hospital was formally opened by King George V and Queen Mary on 12 July 1933, and by His Majesty's authority named the Royal

Masonic Hospital. Queen Elizabeth the Queen Mother opened the new Wakefield Wing of the hospital on 10 December 1958, and also attended the dedication of the hospital chapel.

The Royal Masonic Hospital (RMH) was an independent fee-paying hospital for acute general medicine and surgery. It existed primarily to treat Freemasons and their dependents who travelled to London from all areas of the country. Those who could demonstrate that they were unable to afford the full medical fees were able to apply to the RMH Samaritan Fund for assistance. The RMH began to experience financial difficulties in the 1970s and these deepened in the 1980s. In September 1992 Grand Lodge noted that leave would not be given to the Hospital to appeal for funds and agreed with the Board of General Purposes' feeling that no more time or money should be spent in trying to support the Hospital. In January 1994 the Charity Commissioners appointed a Receiver and Manager to the Hospital, which was subsequently closed in December 1996 and sold in June 1997. The Receiver and Manager was finally discharged in June 2002. However, the spirit and ethos of the Hospital remain alive and well within the work of the Masonic Samaritan Fund.

The Masonic Samaritan Fund (MSF) is the youngest of the major Masonic Charities, having been established as recently as 1990. Until January 2008 it used the working title of New Masonic Samaritan Fund in order to differentiate it from the former RMH Samaritan Fund. 'New' was dropped from its working title at the time it relocated into accommodation within Freemasons' Hall.

It continues to rely on the generosity of individual brethren and their families. Following initial funding from Grand Charity and the Cornwallis Appeal, the Fund only entered the formal Provincial Festival system fully in 2002 – prior to that date further additional financial support had been provided via the London Festival Appeal (£10.6M) and the generosity of the brethren of South Wales Eastern Division (donations totalling £4M). The Fund continues to allocate support to over 500 new applicants each year, at costs in excess of £3M. Since it was established it has already disbursed nearly £40M to more than 8,000 applicants. Despite the continually rising costs of medical treatment, it maintains the boast that no qualifying applicant has ever been turned down through lack of available funds, which is surely a Masonic tradition to be proud of and which deserves to be maintained by continuing Craft support.

The MSF was established to provide support for Freemasons, their wives/widows and dependants who have an identified medical need and who are unable to obtain treatment on the NHS without undue delay or hardship. In recent times this has been extended to include support for dental treatment and respite care. The partners of Freemasons, and the surviving partners of deceased Freemasons, are also eligible.

The Fund welcomes initial enquiries from potential applicants and Almoners at any stage. All applications are dealt with in the strictest confidence. Once the completed application form is returned to the Fund it will be handled by a case administrator and a decision is usually available within 2-4 weeks. The Grants Committee of the MSF meets monthly to ratify all straightforward applications and to consider the more complex ones. The Fund will only support applications received after treatment or care has taken place in exceptional circumstances. An early approach to the Fund is therefore essential.

Further details about the work of the Fund are available from the website. The Fund also produces a newsletter twice a year which is freely available. Speakers are available on request to talk about the support available from the Fund.

### The Charity Festivals
Fund-raising for these charities are mainly via the Provincial festival system, where each of the Provinces (except to date the Metropolitan Grand Lodge) will support each charity in turn, over

about a 45-year cycle. Thus when a festival is ongoing, it has to be remembered that the same charity will not have a major fund-raising drive in the same Province for about another 45 years. And in all of those 45 years, there may be Masons or their families in the Province who are benefiting from that charity annually. And with even the few examples given above of the amounts of money distributed by the charities, it is soon realised that they need every penny that can be raised during each festival to be able to maintain their current standards of care.

The festivals used to last for 7 years, but more recently there have been several Provinces which have opted for a more intensive 4- or 5-year timescale, so that their Masons do not tire from an endless succession of festivals. I recall a senior Provincial Officer visiting a lodge in which the ceiling of the dining room had partially collapsed, and where in the previous week part of the ceiling of the lodge room above had fallen onto the carpet. He noted that the lodge was diverting every pound they could into the festival as it approached the end of the 7 years, which was admirable, but advised them that as soon as the festival had ended they really needed to start the repairs on their building – a stitch in time saves nine, as it were.

# Acknowledgements

I am particularly indebted to the Provinces and lodges who have let me have a sight of their mentoring literature. Many of the themes recur, some of the concepts are individual, and all offered an insight into how different people have thought through the requirements of and for this activity. Included among these are:

The Provinces of Middlesex, Dorset, East Lancashire, Cheshire, Durham, Bedford, Shropshire, West Yorkshire, Somerset and Gloucestershire.

Trinity Lodge No. 254, Coventry; Union Lodge No. 129, Kendal; Wasatch Lodge No. 1, Salt Lake City, Utah; Grand Lodge of California.

I am grateful also to the several people who have proof-read and commented on the text of this book, and especially for the input from James Bartlett. I am pleased that several of the Masonic Charities have actively contributed in this way; including

The Freemasons' Grand Charity;

Edna Darko-Sarkwa of the Royal Masonic Benevolent Institution;

David Ferdinando of the Royal Masonic Trust for Girls and Boys;

Richard Douglas and James Bartlett of the Masonic Samaritan Fund.

And as ever, I must place on record the patience and indulgence of my family and wife Linda while I was immersed in researching for and compiling this book.

**References**
Manchester Association for Masonic Research, Vol 94, 2004, 'Explaining the first degree tracing board'.

**Booklets**
Grand Lodge – *'Freemasonry: an approach to life'*.
Grand Lodge – *'Your questions answered'*.
Peterborough booklets – for the Entered Apprentice, Fellowcraft and Master Mason.
Provincial booklets – covering before joining Freemasonry and after each degree.

**Other books by the same author:**
*'The Assistant Officers – a Practical Guide'* (for Stewards, Tyler, Inner Guard, and Junior and Senior Deacons).
*'The Principal Officers – a Practical Guide'* (for Junior and Senior Wardens, Master and Immediate Past Master).
*'The Secretary and Director of Ceremonies – a Practical Guide'*.
*'The Treasurer, Charity Steward and Almoner – a Practical Guide'*.

*The initial royalties from this book have been given to the East Lancashire 2015 Festival for the Royal Masonic Benevolent Institution.*

# About the Author

Richard Johnson graduated from Cambridge University in 1967 with a BA Honours in Natural Sciences and Metallurgy, and received his MA in 1970; and then was awarded a PhD from Surrey University in 1974 in Materials Science and Metallurgy – all degrees associated with being an 'artificer in metals'.

He was initiated into Salwick Lodge No. 7993 of Preston and West Lancashire in 1983, and became Master in 1992, and was promoted to Past Provincial Junior Grand Deacon in West Lancashire in 1998. He later joined Isaac Newton University Lodge No. 859 of Cambridge in 1999, Blackburn Lodge No. 6720 of Darwen and East Lancashire in 2001, the Manchester Lodge of Masonic Research No. 5502 in 2005, and the Lodge of Unanimity No. 113 in Preston in 2007.

In 2001 he became the founding Master of Brigantes Lodge No. 9734 of Kendal and Cumberland & Westmorland, a lodge created by keen ritualists to perform the long versions of each of the ceremonies – including some of the rarely used items at the backs of the ritual books. In agreeing on the methodology to be adopted in the new lodge, he led some lively discussions about the Craft ritual in a working party, and retains a keen interest in all of the traditional aspects of lodge workings, especially in learning of any unusual ceremonial or lodge jewels that exist. He was appointed to Past Provincial Senior Grand Deacon in this Province in 2003. Since the start of this lodge, he has led the demonstration team of the Brigantes' workings in several formal visits to lodges in England and Scotland, where a selection of those extras have been expounded and explained. From 2006 he has also led a Brigantes' team that has demonstrated the 18th-century workings of an old Cumbrian lodge at venues in England and Scotland, and raising funds for various Masonic and non-Masonic charities.

He has given invited lectures on the development of the early lodges in Lancashire, Cumberland & Westmorland and the North West in general. In 1999 he published a book, Preston Radiant, on the history of the 36 lodges in that city and also covering several of the surrounding lodges in the North West, from their warranting by the different Grand Lodges to the end of the 2nd Millennium. Since then he has written books containing practical advice for the lodge Officers, in particular the Assistant Officers, Principal Officers, Secretary, Director of Ceremonies, Treasurer, Charity Steward and Almoner.

BV - #0008 - 130121 - C0 - 210/150/7 - PB - 9780853183396